An English as an Additional Language (EAL) Programme

You enjoy teaching and, like every other teacher, you want the best for every learner. Recently, you have found a steady stream of learners coming to your school with little or no English. You aren't really sure how to provide the best possible education for them, when they are struggling to understand the English in your already differentiated lessons.

This book provides you with a programme for use as an induction-to-English, complete with integral assessment. It provides guidance on how to bridge the gap between these learners and their peers. It is suitable for learners of any language background (including those not literate in their home language) due to the focus on learning through images. It also includes suggestions on how to include parents who are new to English and ideas on family learning. You'll find an EAL framework to provide structure to your EAL provision across the school, as well as guidance on how to approach class teaching.

Developed from good practice in schools and informed by research, this programme is designed to move learners into English quickly. It uses a visual, structured approach that works alongside immersion in the mainstream.

Caroline Scott has a wealth of experience in supporting young emergent bilingual learners within culturally rich, internationally minded learning environments. Caroline has taught at schools in Europe, Southeast Asia and the Middle East, where she has also trained other teachers in supporting language learning with the curriculum.

Caroline was the founding Head of Primary at a British International school in Cairo, Egypt (a 3–18 IPC school) and the Primary Principal at an International School in Milan, Italy (a 3–18 IB PYP school). She has also held a number of class teaching, EAL coordinator, senior leadership and advisory roles in the UK.

Caroline is the author of *Teaching Children English as an Additional Language: A Programme for 7–11 Year Olds* and *Teaching English as an Additional Language 5–11: A Whole School Resource*. She is the creator of the Learning Village (www.learningvillage.net), an online learning programme for 6–14-year-old English language learners in schools where English is the language of instruction and Community Village (www.communityvillage.net), a blended learning programme for supporting parents who are new-to-English entering English medium schools. Through this programme and her books, she designs resources for learners, as well as training programmes for teachers, to assist them in leading EAL in their school. Caroline is also the editor of the EAL Teaching newsletter, a free monthly EAL newsletter for teachers. She has a keen interest in education technology.

An English as an Additional Language (EAL) Programme

Learning Through Images for 7–14-Year-Olds

Caroline Scott

First published 2020
by Routledge
2 Park Square, Milton Park, Abingdon, Oxon, OX14 4RN

and by Routledge
52 Vanderbilt Avenue, New York, NY 10017

Routledge is an imprint of the Taylor & Francis Group, an informa business

© 2020 Caroline Scott

The right of Caroline Scott to be identified as author of this work has been asserted
by her in accordance with sections 77 and 78 of the Copyright, Designs and
Patents Act 1988.

All rights reserved. The purchase of this copyright material confers the right on the
purchasing institution to photocopy pages which bear the photocopy icon and copyright
line at the bottom of the page. No other parts of this book may be reprinted or reproduced
or utilised in any form or by any electronic, mechanical, or other means, now known or
hereafter invented, including photocopying and recording, or in any information storage
or retrieval system, without permission in writing from the publishers.

Trademark notice: Product or corporate names may be trademarks or registered
trademarks, and are used only for identification and explanation without intent to infringe.

British Library Cataloguing-in-Publication Data
A catalogue record for this book is available from the British Library

Library of Congress Cataloging-in-Publication Data
A catalog record has been requested for this book

ISBN: 978-1-138-50143-0 (hbk)
ISBN: 978-1-138-50146-1 (pbk)
ISBN: 978-1-315-14435-1 (ebk)

Typeset in Bembo
by Apex CoVantage, LLC

Contents

Acknowledgements	vii
Preface	ix

1 An introduction to teaching English as an additional language (EAL) to 7–14-year-olds — 1

The benefits of the programme	2

2 An introduction to the programme — 3

How it works – in theory	3
How it works – in practice (including assessment)	6
Guidance on planning and teaching the programme	9
Creating a successful lesson	16
Non-literate learners	18

3 The programme — 19

The programme overview	19
Induction session contents	19
Induction session details and resources	30
Session 1: Making friends	32
Session 2: Counting 1–20	35
Session 3: Colours and the classroom	37
Session 4: Classroom vocabulary and a/an	41
Session 5: What's that in English?	45
Session 6: His, hers, yours, my	47
Session 7: Numbers 20–50	50
Session 8: Likes and dislikes	51
Session 9: Subject + verb + object	53
Session 10: Animals and plurals	55
Session 11: This, that, these, those	58
Session 12: Imperatives	60
Session 13: Immediate family and have got/has got	62
Session 14: Extended family and possessives	67
Session 15: Description and had got/have got	70
Session 16: Sports and do you like . . . yes, I do/no, I don't	74
Session 17: Can/can't for ability	79
Session 18: Ordinal numbers	81
Session 19: Hobbies	82
Session 20: Have you got . . . ?	84
Session 21: Classifiers	88
Session 22: How much/how many . . .	92
Session 23: Home and there is/are	95
Session 24: Prepositions	101
Session 25: Can/can't for permission	104
Session 26: Do you/does he . . . ?	107
Session 27: Would you like . . . ?	109
Session 28: Feelings	112
Session 29: Shops and places	115
Session 30: Directions	118

4 EAL framework — 127

EAL framework for whole school development	127
Guidance on differentiation for EAL learners in class	131
Suggestions	132
Scaffolding	133
Modes of collaboration	133
Conclusion	136

5 Including families — 137

Family learning	137
Family learning framework	138
English for parents in schools (absolute beginners)	139

Appendix 1	Baseline assessment	145
Appendix 2	Baseline assessment answers	157
Appendix 3	Assessment for learning forms	159

Appendix 4 EAL assessment continuum	163	Glossary	169
		Bibliography	172
		Vocabulary and grammar list	174
Appendix 5 Small-group support record	168	Language structure and vocabulary index	176

Acknowledgements

Thank you to Simon Lobo-Morell, for his understated patience, time, diligence and ongoing support as well as his incredible work on developing the sister programme to this resource (www.learningvillage.net).

Thank you to Helen Adams, Headteacher at Oasis Longmeadow Primary and former EAL Advisor, Vicky Henderson, former teacher, and Yzanne MacKay, editor, for their constructive feedback. Thanks also to Jacqui Holleran, Teacher, for having-a-go and to James Scott for taking part. Also to my incredible family for being so supportive and my Mum. Although she is no longer with us, her profound impact on my life and work continues.

Special thanks to all the staff at Wood End Academy, St John's C of E Primary School, Tudor Primary School, Lea Forest Academy, Cairo English Schooland the International School of Milan.

Thank you to the London Borough of Tower Hamlets for the Innovations Funding which allowed me to get my original programme started all those years ago. This support has given me the momentum to continue to develop it over the past years.

Thank you to Annette Rook, my former headteacher, who allowed me the freedom to develop my interests and inspired me to follow this path.

Thanks also to Sobia Zaman, Across Cultures Content Developer, and Heidi Niederkofler, Across Cultures Admin, Laura Haines, EAL Coordinator, International School of Milan, Sally Flannagan, Mother Tongue Coordinator, International School of Milan, Terry Haywood, Former Headmaster, International School of Milan, Ragini Patel, Tudor Primary, Heather Day, EAL Advisor, Vicki Wilson, EAL Team Leader, Yew Chung International Primary School, Norm Dean, Deputy Director, Yew Chung International Primary School, Rachel Parsons, EAL/SEN Teacher, Bradford Girls School, Sharmila Shah, EAL, Bradford Girls School, Amy Tilson, OCT, Academie Ste Cecile International School, Canada, Nick Parkes, English Support Teacher, Heidelberg International School, Germany, Rebecca Richardson, School Leader, Bradford Girls School, Michelle Wain, Ethnic Minority Achievement Adviser, Havering, Sue Crane, Ethnic Minority Achievement Consultant, Tower Hamlets Ethnic Minority Acheivement, Ann Cobden, former Deputy Head, Wood End Academy, Warner Stainbank, Headteacher, Wood End Academy, Anne Hayes, Previous Headteacher, Wood End Academy, Jasminder Manku, EAL Teaching Assistant, Wood End Academy, Terry Bennett, Headteacher, St John's C or E Primary School, Angela Vasey, Inclusion Coordinator, St John's C or E Primary School, Hilary Thompson, former Headteacher, Lea Forest Academy, Sarah Jones, EAL Coordinator, Lea Forest Academy, Sarah Brown, previous Head of International Primary Curriculum (IPC) and IB Curriculum Manager, Coreen Seers, EAL Consultant & Author, Independent. Tom George, Director, Happy Hour, Sue Scott, Advisor, Lindsay Hunter, Solicitor, Owen White, Mentor, formerly Edtech Futures, Adam Sefton, former Director, Reading Room, among many others who have all played a part in supporting and piloting my work in various capacities and therefore supporting the development of this book. I have been very lucky to have such supportive people around me.

Preface

I originally began writing this book as a replacement for *Teaching English as an Additional Language: A Programme for 7–11 Year Olds*. The book was becoming dated: it included references to the old National Curriculum, former assessment continua and outdated resources. As it is a popular, well-used resource also being used widely for learners up to 14-year-olds despite its original focus on 7-11 year olds, I decided to give the book an overhaul. By widening the age range, removing the resources section, introducing a new, much-needed summary of on differentiation in class, some guidance on family learning as well as a summary of provision across the school, I felt the book's core would remain the same. I also felt just a simple upgrade of the illustrations to colour photographs (a common request from those using the programme) wouldn't make too much difference.

However, in my usual way, I ended up overhauling the entire book, looking for ways to ensure that learners remained focused and efficient in their learning. On reflection, while very useful for induction-to-English, the programme could allow the teacher and learners to stray from quick, focused support to a more relaxed, slower teaching methodology. The programme included a variety of activities to engage learners, in a way that didn't have an excessive focus on speaking and listening activities and thus often led to a greater amount of time being spent on reading and writing activities. There is definitely a place for this kind of programme; however, I didn't feel this was the best I could offer.

Over the years, I have worked with and monitored many learners undertaking the 7–11 programme in a variety of schools. They have made good progress.

> We have used Caroline's approach to teaching English as an additional language for some years now and it has been particularly successful with newly arrived pupils at Key Stage 2 who are early stage learners of English. . . . Schools in Tower Hamlets who have used Caroline's programme have reported good progress for their pupils.
>
> (Tower Hamlets Ethnic Minority Achievement Service, London)

For the last five years, alongside the development of an online learning programme (www.learningvillage.net), I have developed these methods further to allow a learner to focus on learning key vocabulary and language structures more efficiently, whilst still providing ample opportunity for speaking and listening and applying learning.

I feel strongly that if learners are to be withdrawn from a class, or given extra classes to support learning everyday language, a programme of learning should fulfil a few vital criteria:

1   Build confidence and friendships.
2   Engage the learners in interesting, functional, appropriate speaking and listening activities.
3   Teach learners how to learn independently.
4   Connect speaking and listening to reading and writing.
5   Teach learners valuable everyday language.
6   Align to the curriculum, where possible.

In this new book, I have evolved the programme to focus on these elements:

1. Build confidence and friendships.
   When learners join together as a group and learn collaboratively, we observe them relaxing and enjoying learning the vocabulary and language structures through speaking and listening games. Concern about getting the language right (often a challenging and nerve-wracking experience when speaking in a new language for the first time) becomes secondary to the joy and engagement of the collaboration. It also results in connecting learners who are in the same position.

2. Engage the learners in interesting, functional, appropriate speaking and listening activities.
   As each lesson is built on collaborative learning games, speaking and listening is integral to the learning experience. Designed to remove unfocused learning, this evolved methodology is centred on learning a small amount of key vocabulary, and a few language structures, to help learners immediately articulate their needs through speaking and listening activities. It also allows learners of any language background, including those not literate in their home language, to access lessons through an image-based approach and identification of initial letter sounds matched to images.

3. Teach learners how to learn independently.
   In the new programme, sessions concentrate on introducing vocabulary and language structures in a focused method: showing, hiding and recalling the language (alongside reading) and using it immediately. Through this clear method of learning (including translating to the learner's own language), we can support learners in developing their own learning tools. When we model the methodology, we provide learners with the skills to help themselves learn independently.

4. Connect speaking and listening to reading and writing.
   Teachers often struggle to include learners whose script is unwritten, whose language is less common and harder to source in translation, or who aren't yet literate in their home language. When we learn through images, however, we use a global language. The new programme's speaking and listening activities lead to a short, focused reading and writing activity at the end of each lesson. Writing is clearly concentrated on one application of one sentence related to the key vocabulary of the lesson. For non-literate learners, the focus can be on initial letters or single words.

5. Teach learners valuable everyday language.
   An induction-to-English teaches and supports learners in learning everyday language; through this, we naturally value and encourage that learning. It's easy for the focus of learning to be on the technical language that goes with the curriculum, rather than some of the everyday language that can be more appropriate in the early days of learning.

6. Align to the curriculum, where possible.
   The small-group support provided during induction-to-English can often be linked to content of the curriculum and potential links should always be made priority, e.g., a topic on keeping healthy brings perfect opportunities to learn vocabulary or language structures on food, types of sports or parts of the body (all of which are included in this programme). Teachers can choose to insert their own additional relevant topics by using their own flashcards with the suggested methodology.

In summary, as an induction-to-English may require a learner to miss out on other learning (for a short, limited time period) or require them to learn in addition to their usual studies, the learning must be well-focused, effective and immediately functional, as well as enjoyable, to raise learners' confidence and build friendships. This new programme is designed to deliver this.

The sessions are intended to offer a springboard for learning further English. For more resources and an even more comprehensive sister programme, it's worth exploring the Learning Village (www.learningvillage.net), which works seamlessly alongside this programme. The Learning Village follows the same sessions and format of learning, but with extended vocabulary for every lesson and a continuation of the programme, as well as a phonics and curriculum language offerings. The two resources are designed to work together, increasing learners' ability to support themselves, as well as providing an engaging teacher platform for induction-to-English, gap-filling and pre-teaching of vocabulary and language structures before they happen in the curriculum.

I do hope you enjoy working with the programme. Please get in touch with any feedback: caroline@axcultures.com. For more information on the impact of the methodology outlined in this Preface and also used in the Learning Village, see these case studies: www.learningvillage.net/casestudy.

An introduction to teaching English as an additional language (EAL) to 7–14-year-olds

"Teachers should plan teaching opportunities to help pupils develop their English and should aim to provide the support pupils need to take part in all subjects."

(National Curriculum, 2014)

This is a fundamental expectation in schools where English is the language of instruction. Often, due to high levels of international migration, pupils' levels of English as an Additional Language (EAL) in the classroom range from absolute beginner to fluent, and teachers therefore take on the challenge of differentiating for language learning alongside content learning. They have the difficult task of providing all students with depth of learning in a range of content across the curriculum despite learners' English proficiency level. This limited English proficiency is often a barrier to learning: "English language learners' lack of oral language proficiency has often hindered their opportunity to receive cognitively stimulating and content-level appropriate instruction in school" (Carrasquillo, Kucer and Abrams, 2004, 30).

Using mother tongue to support conceptual learning is a crucial part of initial access to curriculum content as it can assist learners in comprehending content in their own language. Once comprehension occurs in one's own language, the content is transferable to the new language (Cummins, 2000), learners just need the vocabulary with corresponding language structures to articulate their learning.

Although they need to continue using both languages to support their bilingual development, learners require a fast, effective, consistent approach to learning English. Supporting newcomers in learning Basic Interpersonal

Communication Skills (BICS; sometimes termed as social language) (Cummins, 2000) can provide opportunities for success in using the meaningful English language required for day-to-day conversations, as well as to build confidence. If learning is provided in a small-group setting, it increases the opportunities for leaners to access teacher support and allows teachers to provide more bespoke learning experience.

Research undertaken in England, Canada and the USA highlighted the general features of EAL learners' situation in schools. These included students served by educational systems, which claim to be inclusive, yet do not offer the full range of their language and learning needs required for learners (Mohan, Leung and Davison, 2001). Perhaps, in many countries, like England, it is due to national oversight in EAL policy and procedure: The most potentially damaging feature of EAL policy in England is the absence of any national oversight or provision of professional qualifications, staff development and specialist roles for teachers and other school staff working with children with EAL (Hutchinson, 2018).

Despite this, teachers continue to deliver support for learners, tirelessly, in many ways. In the face of a lack of external support (funding, training, resources, etc.), the time it can take to undertake adequate differentiation can appear to be a mammoth task. This programme is designed to offer a practical, easy-to-follow methodology, offering a clear initial pathway for supporting teachers of new-to-English learners in the English-speaking mainstream.

As we provide learners with appropriate opportunities to be successful at using English in context, they can make increased progress in immediate language learning needs, build confidence in English and reduce the language gap between them and their peers. Be mindful that this process will take time and learners will need ongoing English language support to ensure they have the academic language proficiency needed to be successful with their studies. Cummins (2002) outlines the requirement for both Basic Interpersonal Communication Skills (BICS) and Cognitive Academic Language Proficiency (CALP).

> It takes on average five to seven years to become fully competent in a second language, although individuals will vary in the speed with which they acquire this competence. Fluency in spoken English is usually achieved within two years but the ability to read and understand more complex texts containing unfamiliar cultural references and to write the academic language needed for success in examinations takes much longer.
>
> (Cummins, 2000)

This programme is built on the principles of teaching and learning outlined in the National Curriculum for England (2014) "Teachers should set high expectations for every pupil." The Curriculum also sets national expectations for EAL learners:

- Teachers must also take account of the needs of pupils whose first language is not English. Monitoring of progress should take account of child's age, length of time in the country, previous educational experience and ability in other languages.
- The ability of pupils whom English is an additional language to take part in the national curriculum may be in advance of their communication skills in English. Teachers should plan teaching opportunities to help pupils develop their English and should aim to provide the support pupils need to take part in all subjects."

Learners should always be encouraged to use their main languages in learning to support their bilingual development. "Two languages work together to improve understanding" Gallagher (2008). Special attention must be given to instigate connections with learners' mother tongue, where possible, during every lesson of this programme and links made to the curriculum to engage and include learners as much as possible in learning from the curriculum.

The benefits of the programme

This programme includes:

- Instructions and resources for teaching fundamental grammar and vocabulary needed to speak English
- Initial baseline assessment as well as ongoing tracking and feedback
- Integral speaking and listening
- Activities that are fun and collaborative
- A suggested setting for building confidence and creating friendships
- Emergency language sessions to support the learner in the first two to three days
- Opportunities for self-study and home learning through a 'Remember Book'
- Support for the learner's mother tongue
- Revision of recently learned English, which forms a key part of every lesson
- Cross-curricular links and opportunities for excursions
- Opportunities to practise the language through applying learning to real-life situations
- A wealth of carefully tailored flashcards to support learning, including a framework for whole school EAL development
- A clear, easy to use, consistent format
- A selection of language learning strategies to empower learners

This programme has a flexible approach to assessment, planning, teaching and learning in order to ensure that adaptation is made appropriately for EAL learners' needs. It has been based on tried and tested research. The first version of the programme was introduced in Lawdale Junior School in Tower Hamlets, London, and later used in other schools within the borough and beyond. In 2012, a sister programme was released, Teaching English as an Additional Language 5–11: A whole school resource, and in 2016, an online evolution of the books (Learning Village, www.learningvillage.net) was launched to allow learners and teachers to enjoy the benefits using it as a blended learning tool (a tool that provides integrated online and offline learning opportunities) that allows for independent as well as teacher support sessions across all curriculum areas with embedded assessment. The Learning Village compliments this book. For more information on the impact of the methodology used in the book, integral to the Learning Village, see: www.learningvillage.net/casestudy.

If you would like more information about this programme or any related programmes, please take a look at the Across Cultures website, www.axcultures.com, or contact the author at caroline@axcultures.com.

2

An introduction to the programme

How it works – in theory

This induction programme (also known as a withdrawal, pull-out, intervention or small-group new-to-English programme) offers initial English support for learners arriving in the English-speaking mainstream with little or no English. Although learners should be present in most mainstream lessons, they can attend this small-group induction class regularly (up to five lessons a week). It is designed to help learners to access some of the basic functional English language they need in a welcoming small-group setting whilst providing opportunities for learners to feel confident and ready to take risks in language learning. It is designed to support newcomers in feeling safe, settled, valued and a sense of belonging.

Lileikienė and Danilevičienė (2016) found that learners felt uncomfortable feelings when learning or using a new language. They proved that this anxiety was a powerful predictor for demotivation in language learning and impeded the acquisition of the new language. The research analysis also revealed that the majority of younger respondents demonstrated a higher degree of anxiety. This programme is designed to boost learner confidence in using the language they need to access school life by offering appropriately levelled, relevant content which is fun, engaging and social for learners with similar levels of English. It acts as a bridge for learners with very limited English to initially: 'kickstart' students' learning of English and to offer them collective support during their early days and months in an English-medium environment (Sears, 2015).

If teachers are required to raise the level of attainment in the curriculum, they need to provide learners with the tools to access the learning. "Separate or some kind of 'sheltered' instruction may also be the best option for recently arrived English language learners" (Gibbons, 2009; also see Carrasquillo and Rodriguez, 2002).

This is a flexible programme that can be taught by an EAL (English as an Additional Language) teacher, class teacher or teaching assistant. It requires regular small-group or one-to-one lessons. It should be based on each student's needs and offered in short sessions that focus on progress in learning the vocabulary and language structures to access simple conversations with their teachers and peers. The programme is effective for finely-tuned, time-limited support which supports the needs of individuals and groups of learners, following a baseline assessment and ongoing assessment for learning (see Appendices 2 and 3 for supporting assessment resources). It works seamlessly with its sister programme the Across Cultures, Learning Village (www.learningvillage.net), which offers additional content for beginner to intermediate learners. Additionally, it contains next steps for learners who have completed this programme, alongside phonics and technical or academic language needed to access the curriculum.

The national curriculum states that, "Pupils' acquisition and command of vocabulary are key to their learning and progress across the curriculum. Teachers should therefore develop vocabulary actively, building systematically on pupils' current knowledge" (National Curriculum of England, 2014).

The programme focusses on vocabulary and language structures that reflect the real-life needs of learners. Learners use new vocabulary which they then insert into meaningful language structures (which often have a grammatical focus). It is a form-focused approach. The emphasis is on communication through the use of the newly introduced language structures and vocabulary that are presented. Courses with a form-focused component achieve better results than courses without such a component. The important issue is to achieve a balance between meaning-focused activities, form-focused activities, and fluency development activities (Nation, 1997). There is growing evidence that learners in content-based programmes such as French immersion [*similarly English immersion*] need more opportunities to focus on form and receive corrective feedback (Lightbrown and Spada, 2013).

The programme offers a well-structured cycle of learning that includes significant opportunities for speaking and listening activities through collaboration and games with their peers. Its duration is based on a learner's understanding of the vocabulary and language structures presented.

In the case of very limited to zero exposure to the language, "pre-induction flashcard resources" have been included in the programme to introduce new, useful communication methods to learners before the main programme begins.

Strategic, self-regulated language learning

> Oxford (2011) outlines strategic, self-regulated language learning as a deliberate, goal directed attempt to manage and control efforts to learn the foreign or second language. Such a strategy is a broad, teachable action that learners choose from among alternatives and employ for language learning strategies.
>
> (Afflerbach, Pearson and Paris, 2008)

There has been significant discussion in recent times about how to support learners with their learning.

> Strategic, self-regulated learning lies at the heart of second/foreign language acquisition. Over decades, we have seen applied linguistics suggesting the right amount of comprehensible input, opportunities for output, correct feedback, task-based presentation, and contextual scaffolding in the classroom. But after all this, the only thing teachers can do is to wait and hope that learners will notice the patterns or automatically activate their implicit learning mechanisms. While this might happen, the central thesis behind language learning strategy research is that learners, supported by teachers and curricula, can play a much more active role in managing and controlling the learning process, thereby maximizing the outcomes of learning. Instruction in strategic learning can result in better learners.
>
> (Gu 2010, 1)

Through the use of a Remember Book (see "How it works – in practice") and through modelling a number of games to learn new vocabulary and language structures both independently and with their peers or parents, we can coach learners into taking strategic ownership of their learning in this way.

A study by López-Vargas, Ibáñez-Ibáñez and Racines-Prada (2017) also indicated that, "learning achievement was significantly greater in students that used the metacognitive scaffolding in comparison to the achievement of their classmates that did not."

Learners in schools have the dual goal of learning content and language, so learning the new language is an additional barrier over native speakers. If a teacher can instigate the learners' use of strategic, self-regulated language learning, then they can be more efficient at supporting themselves.

A cycle of learning

The learning cycle is designed to offer a clear approach to learning new vocabulary and language structures quickly and effectively. The titles used later: connection, activation, demonstration and consolidation, stem from the 4 Stage Accelerated Learning Cycle (Smith, Lovatt and Wise, 2003). The cycle is also adapted from a synthesized inquiry cycle that combines the strengths of existing inquiry-based learning frameworks (Pedaste et al., 2015), for example, orientate (connect), explore (activate), refine (demonstrate) and reflect (consolidate) as referenced later. It also links to Gibbon's (2009) teaching and learning cycle, for example, building the field (connect), modelling genre (activate), joint construction (demonstrate) and independent writing (consolidate). Additionally, it is based on research by Nation (1997), who states, "For fast vocabulary expansion, however, it [learning through context which is small and cumulative] is not sufficient by itself." This cycle of learning works with a vocabulary/language structure learning programme designed to move learners into English quickly. It is one resource that will support learners, it will be used alongside guided reading, phonics and differentiated immersion in the mainstream.

Connection

> Students must have a model – a network of related ideas about the material – not just isolated facts. . . . This process involves connecting the new material to prior knowledge.
>
> (Zadina, 2014)

At the beginning of a session the connection phase (orientate, assess and build the field) allows the learners to orientate themselves with the context and start building their understanding of the new topic. It also allows both learners and teachers to collaboratively assess the learner's understanding.

Activation

The activation phase (explore, modelling and joint construction) is for generating ideas on how you use the language. It incorporates modelling and joint construction.

Demonstration

The demonstration phase (refine, practice and move to independence) helps the learners to recall and use the vocabulary or language structures independently.

Consolidation

The consolidation phase (revise, apply and reflect) is a chance for learners to revisit as well as reflect on their learning and to relate the learning to their own lives by applying it to real life experiences.

See 'Guidance on planning and teaching the programme' for a full break down of the learning cycle for the induction.

This cycle has also been applied to teaching in the mainstream (see 'EAL framework,' Chapter 4).

Since learning new everyday language is not usually the same as teaching curriculum concepts that require higher order thinking, the cycle of learning can be short and structured, focusing efficiently on memorizing, practicing and applying new language that can later be used to engage in higher order thinking. Even so, there can still be elements of engaging learners in thinking for themselves during certain parts of the learning cycle. This could occur, for example, during the connection phase, where learners decipher the image, or during activation, when they use the language they learnt for one image to decipher the language they need for other similar images. Then, during consolidating they can think for themselves by using the new language learnt to different contexts. They can also begin self-regulating in the demonstration phase by choosing known games to help them learn and

then reflecting on their progress or in the consolidation phase by using the Remember Book.

Reviewing learning

Revisiting learning is important for consolidation of learning. Learners should spend a large part of the lesson revising what they learned in a previous lesson (strategies used to revise learning might include applying the learning from their Remember Book [see 'How it works – in practice (including assessment)], responding to learners' questions or repeating practice sessions from a previous lesson they enjoyed or found challenging. Teachers mustn't be afraid to explore a variety of ways to engage with using the new language taught ". . . use multiple pathways when teaching, practicing, and assessing. See it, say it, model it, apply it, draw it, analogize it and so forth" (Zadina, 2014).

Cross-curricular links

> Opportunities are offered to 'plan teaching opportunities to help pupils develop their English and should aim to provide the support pupils need to take part in all subjects.'
> (National Curriculum for England, 2014)

In order to practise and apply learning as well as support learners in accessing the content-based learning objectives demanded by the curriculum, there are some suggested cross-curricular links (see 'Induction session contents,' pp. 19-21).

Excursions are also an easy way to link learning to the curriculum. They are not only an opportunity to apply learners' new language in context, but also offer a rich linguistic and cultural learning experience and a chance for learners to ask questions. This is especially important when some new arrivals may have never experienced day-to-day outings like this in their new country. An excursion offers another way of helping them acclimatize to their new environment and form friendships.

Suggestions for excursions:

- ▪ Pre-induction session – A tour round school to practice the place names and general orientation
- ▪ Session 29 – A town to practise places and shops, directions, prepositions, where is/are . . .?
- ▪ Session 27 – A visit to the school canteen to ask for food

If excursions are not an option, then role play should be heavily integrated in learning.

Assessment

Baseline and formative assessment underpins the programme. This is based on findings from research conducted by Black and William (1998b). They identified that:

- Pupils need effective feedback
- Pupils need to be actively involved in their own learning
- Teachers need to take account of assessment in order to inform teaching
- Teachers have enormous influence on the motivation of pupils
- There is a need for pupils to assess themselves

William (2011) points out formative assessment "is a process," which means feedback given on a test doesn't really fall into this category.

How it works – in practice (including assessment)

This is a short, flexible programme which provides lessons and resources for an adult to teach English as an additional language to individuals or small groups of learners. Learning is based on assessment (see "Assessment", p. 8). If learners have grasped some of the vocabulary and language structures already, the programme will be shorter.

Each set of lessons is called a 'session'. A session is a topic which includes a number of lessons. The teacher of the programme should use the baseline assessment (see Appendix 2) as a summative guide to learner starting points. Each question links to a corresponding session. At the end of each lesson, the teacher reassesses the learners by making a note on the Assessment for Learning Form (see Appendix 3). This then informs teachers of learners' areas of difficulty which can be built into revision sections of future lessons. Teachers should use their judgment to keep the programme well-paced and progressive

Before the programme commences, it is important that newcomers to English have some way of communicating. Teachers can provide some priority language flashcards (with English and space to write their mother tongue) for communicating some of the very basics. (See Chapter 3 – pre-induction flashcards, pp. 22–27). The learner can use these pictures or statements by showing or pointing to what they need. Teachers should set aside some time for a buddy, parents, mentor, teaching assistant or teacher to introduce these pre-induction flashcards before they begin class.

At the end of this programme, learners should be proficient in some of the basics of English. This does not mean that they should be expected to achieve at the same level as their peers, but rather that the class teacher will be able to differentiate for the EAL learner more easily in mainstream lessons and learners will have greater confidence in articulating themselves at a basic level. The learners will also have a good foundation to build on in order to close the gap between themselves and their peers.

The Remember Book

A Remember Book (a small notebook) can assist the teachers in supporting learners with controlling their cognitive strategy use (the language learning strategies they use to help them learn). It is designed to support learners in acquiring and practising their learning independently.

The Remember Book forms a large part of the students' learning in this programme. Throughout the course, the learners should write, update and revise new learning in the book in order to practise their learning.

The Remember Book has two functions.

1. To provide a record of what learners have learned at the end of every lesson in order to support revision of English outside the class.
2. To record independent learning in order to provide opportunities for understanding new learning in lessons and then revising the new language outside the class.

Teachers can present the vocabulary or language structures on the board at the start of the lesson. Learners can write the new language at the end of the lesson once they have practised the learning outcome.

Learners must take their Remember Book and a pencil with them to lessons and be encouraged to write words or sentences in the back of the book as soon as they learn useful language. If learners are literate in a home language, then they should be encouraged to write the translation. If not, they can stick in associated flashcard images alongside the vocabulary or language structure to remind themselves. In cases where the learner is not literate, learning through images is very appropriate. However, learners will require additional phonics support during a lesson by using initial letter sounds to match words to images. This supports the learner with the first steps in associating sounds with text. Spelling isn't important at this stage – it's the speaking, listening and remembering that is important. The attention to detail in the spelling can come later. Learners use the back of the book for their independently learnt words and the new language learnt in lessons can be positioned at the front of the book.

Each page should be folded into two. For example:

Home language	English
_____	_____
_____	_____
_____	_____
_____	_____

Page 1

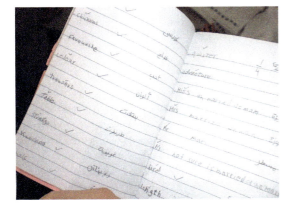

Figure 2.1 Example Remember Book

Learners can use the Remember Book independently by:

- Adding new words at the back
- Folding the page so they can't see the English and use their translations to look, cover, say and check that they remember the new word
- Ticking off words they know and highlighting words they find difficult
- Copying out the new learning on to post-it notes which they can stick on the wall and learn. These post-it notes could be stuck randomly around the house on specific objects as a label of what it is or put in key places where the learners spend time; for example, next to the bed, by the TV or at the back of the front door

Learners can use the Remember Book with a parent or friend by:

- The parent or friend reading the word in the home language and then the learner saying it in English
- The parent or friend reading the word in English and the learner saying it in the home language
- The learner reading the words aloud for the parent or friend who can then check their pronunciation
- The parent or friend giving the learner five words a day from the book in the morning to be reviewed throughout the day

The Remember Book should form part of the learner's homework and can become part of the daily homework routine. The work they focus on in their Remember Book will ensure that they are surrounded by language in school and at home. This will motivate them, help them to identify what they need to learn and support progression.

Assessment

Baseline assessment

Each learner needs to take the baseline assessment (see Appendices 1 and 2) in order to help the teacher understand the learner's needs. This assessment will allow the teacher to decide, first, if the programme would be suitable for the learner and, second, how to place the learner quickly and accurately on to the appropriate sessions. Be aware that learners may not have seen an assessment like this and may not be able to answer the questions even though they know the English.

Therefore, careful thought must be given to how and what assessment questions are to be verbally asked or explained. If learners struggle to complete the assessment, allow them to leave it unfinished. It's more important they feel successful than they complete an assessment.

Assessment for learning

At the end of every lesson, each learner's understanding of the session is assessed using an Assessment for Learning form. This is populated by the teacher who assesses each learner's performance during the lesson. It should then be used to inform teacher planning (see Appendix 3). It is advisable that the teacher has the Assessment for Learning form with them during the lesson in order to update as they observe the learners' achievements.

The Assessment for Learning forms require the use of a triangle Δ to show the level of understanding each learner has of the learning intention. A one-sided triangle next to the learner's name would mean they don't understand and the new learning needs to be revisited. A two-sided triangle would mean they almost understand and may need a little more consolidation to fully grasp the concept. A fully drawn triangle would mean that the learner understands the new learning and is ready to move on. This Assessment for Learning form should be used to plan the revision sessions. The areas learners find difficult should be revisited regularly so that the learning is consolidated. Upon grasping the concept, the Assessment for Learning form needs to be updated.

Any method could be used to collect this assessment information. For example:

- Observations
- Marking
- Questioning
- Learner self-assessment

Learner self-assessment

It is strongly recommended that learners self-assess their learning. If students are involved in assessing their needs, they can be actively involved in deciding what they need to learn next. Self-assessment is very motivating for learners and helps them to take responsibility for their own learning.

Some methods of learner self-assessment:

- Ask learners to show how much they understand the learning challenge by showing their hand with a number of fingers that reflects how much they understand. For example, five fingers shows they understand, three fingers means they think they understand, no fingers means they don't understand.
- Ask learners to draw a face under the work they complete in their Remember Book or on the Assessment for Learning form that reflects how much they understand the learning intention. For example, a ☺ means they understand, a straight-lined face :-/ means they think they understand, and ☹ means they do not understand.
- Ask learners to tell you how much they understand the learning challenge. For example, I understand how to. . ., I think I understand how to. . ., or I don't understand how to.. . .
- The learners can use traffic light colours to signify understanding. For instance, showing red means learners don't understand, yellow/orange means they aren't sure and green means they understand.
- Learners can show thumbs up if they understand and thumbs down if they don't.

Assessment using an EAL assessment continuum

An EAL assessment continuum can be used as an overview of a learner's progress in EAL over time (see Appendix 4 for Reading and Viewing and Writing continuums of The Bell Foundation's EAL Assessment Framework for Schools, which is available free to download: www.bell-foundation.org.uk/eal-programme/teaching-resources/eal-assessment-framework/ and NASSEA EAL Framework, www.nassea.org.uk/eal-assessment-framework/) which has a small charge.

Both frameworks start from absolute beginner and track a learner through to the advanced levels of proficiency. This kind of tracking should show learners progressing and should highlight particular needs, barriers to learning or significant progress that might not otherwise have been identified. Other learner assessments like the baseline assessment (Appendix 1), phonics, reading, unaided writing samples and any other assessments can help you populate the continuum so that progress is tracked over time. Teachers should highlight and date the time the learners achieved a learning challenge each term.

Some schools in England and Wales are also using EAL Proficiency codes which grade learners from A-E. Note that they are not a replacement for an EAL assessment continuum which contains greater detail.

Code Description

A – New to English

May use first language for learning and other purposes. May remain completely silent in the classroom. May be copying/repeating some words or phrases. May understand some everyday expressions in English but may have minimal or no literacy in English. Needs a considerable amount of EAL support.

B – Early acquisition

May follow day-to-day social communication in English and participate in learning activities with support. Beginning to use spoken English for social purposes. May understand simple instructions and can follow narrative/ accounts with visual support. May have developed some skills in reading and writing. May have become familiar with some subject specific vocabulary. Still needs a significant amount of EAL support to access the curriculum.

C – Developing competence

May participate in learning activities with increasing independence. Able to express self orally in English, but structural inaccuracies are still apparent. Literacy will require ongoing support, particularly for understanding text and writing. May be able to follow abstract concepts and more complex written English. Requires ongoing EAL support to access the curriculum fully.

D – Competent

Oral English will be developing well, enabling successful engagement in activities across the curriculum. Can read and understand a wide variety of texts. Written English may lack complexity and contain occasional evidence of errors in structure. Needs some support to access subtle nuances of meaning, to refine English usage, and to develop abstract vocabulary. Needs some/occasional EAL support to access complex curriculum material and tasks.

E – Fluent

Can operate across the curriculum to a level of competence equivalent to that of a pupil who uses English as his/her first language. Operates without EAL support across the curriculum (Department for Education, 2015).

Guidance on planning and teaching the programme

This programme has been designed to make the teacher the expert. Teachers can make reference to the programme in order to enhance what they teach and adapt their planning and teaching so it is appropriate for the learner.

Before any learning begins, the learners should take the baseline assessment (see Appendix 1). The assessment is designed to highlight learning requirements in the learner's basic vocabulary and language structures on commencement of the programme. It can be revisited termly as a summative assessment to check progress.

If you wish to extend the programme, you can source an extended version in the sister programme, Learning Village (www.learningvillage.net), which offers additional content for beginner to intermediate learners as well as next steps for learners who have completed this programme alongside phonics and curriculum language.

Use the lesson flashcard resources with the following cycles of learning. Session can be learner-directed or teacher-supported.

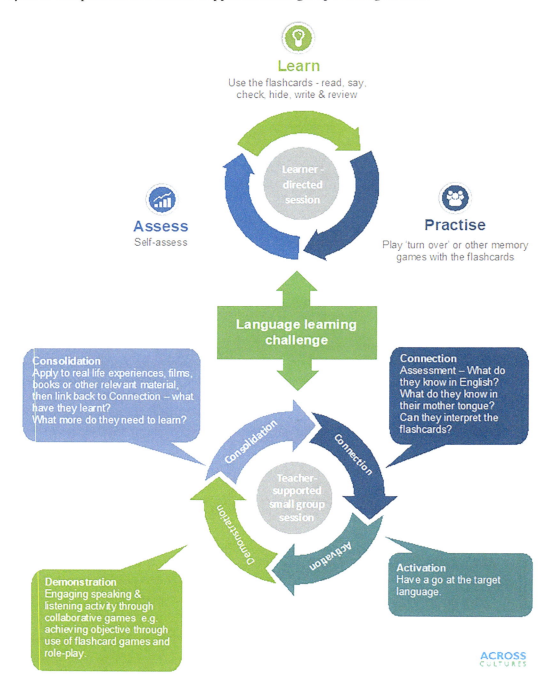

Figure 2.2 Supporting EAL learners in small groups, EAL Framework: Strand 4
Source: www.axcultures.com/framework

Cycle of learner-directed learning – further detail:

Cycle of independent learning sessions – Part 1

Figure 2.3 Cycle independent learning sessions. Supporting EAL learners in small groups, EAL Framework: Strand 4
Source: www.axcultures.com/framework

Session breakdown	Explanation
Review – Use of flashcard resources from previous lessons	This is a review of what they know. The learner uses previously learnt flashcards without words. One by one they turn them over and say the vocabulary or language structures associated with the flashcard. If they know them then they should move on, if not then they can refer to the answer, hide it and try again.
Assess – Use of flashcard resources for a new lesson	Learners look at the images briefly with the text then they remove the text and have a go at saying the words or language structures. If they know them and are confident using the language they should move to a new set of flashcards. If they aren't sure they should continue to the next step of learning the flashcards.
Learn	Learners look at the images (presented with text), translate in their head to ensure they know the meaning then say the word in English. They then refer to the images without text and say the corresponding vocabulary or language structures again to check they can recall it. If they don't remember it, they can look at the text again to remind themselves. They should continue this until they can remember all the vocabulary or language structures.
Practice	Learners need to continue to remember the vocabulary or language structures. They can do this through regular use of the flashcards. Provide them with some independent methods of learning to use. Methods of learning: 1. Look, cover, say, check – independent (use the Remember Book for this) 2. Turn-over – independent (see 'Collaborative games for the demonstration phase' for instructions on the turnover game, pp. 6-7)

© Caroline Scott (2020), *An English as an Additional Language (EAL) Programme:
Learning Through Images for 7–14-Year-Olds*, Routledge

Cycle of teacher-supported small-group learning sessions – Part 2

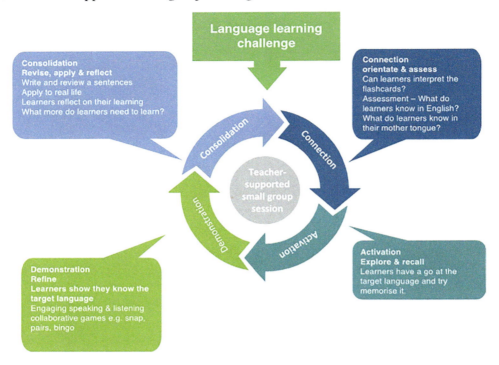

Figure 2.4 Cycle of teacher-supported small-group learning sessions. Supporting EAL learners in small groups, EAL Framework: Strand 4 www.axcultures.com/framework

If you are choosing a vocabulary lesson follow option A. If you are choosing a language structure lesson follow option B (see lessons and resources in Chapter 3). These lessons should be pacey. Prepare the flashcard resources before you start the lesson.

Option A: Vocabulary lesson (learning words, e.g. a mouse)

Prepare the flashcard resources before you start the lesson (see chapter 3)

Session breakdown	*Explanation*
Review – Use of flashcard resources from previous lessons	This is a review of a previous session. The teacher or learner can plan for this by using the vocabulary/language structure learning games from previous sections, e.g., a snap flashcard game practicing can/can't. (also see Collaborative games for the demonstrate phase pp. 15-16)
Connection (orientate & assess) – Use of flashcard resources for a new lesson	The connection phase allows the learners to orientate themselves with the context. **Orientate:** Choose 1–2 vocabulary or language structure lesson flashcards (without the text). Ask: 'What can you tell me about these pictures?' Learners can answer in English or in their home language. **Assess:** This also allows both learners and teachers to collaboratively assess understanding and make judgments on what learners need to know: Do they understand the picture? Can they say it in their home language? Can they say it in English?

© Caroline Scott (2020), *An English as an Additional Language (EAL) Programme: Learning Through Images for 7–14-Year-Olds*, Routledge

Session breakdown	Explanation
Activation (explore & recall)	The activation phase is for generating ideas on how you use the pictured language and having a go at using it. **Explore the images** (to support comprehension): Ensure you have copied the vocabulary lesson flashcard resources (if required for the lesson) and cut out all the pictures and text. Ask the learners to guess which text goes with which picture and match the image to text themselves. If the learners need further help, match the vocabulary to the text together. However, encourage the learners to try themselves first.
	Recall (to support memorizing): Say the corresponding text for each flashcard. Ask the learners to repeat it. Remove the text from one flashcard and ask the learners to recall it. Then repeat them all together again. Remove the text from a second flashcard and ask the learners to recall both those flashcards without text then repeat them all together again. Continue until the learners are confident in saying all the vocabulary without the text prompts.
Demonstration (refine)	**Show they know the target language:** Help the learners to recall the vocabulary by providing a method of learning (learners can choose their most effective learning method once they know the games): Choose one of the methods of learning (see 'Collaborative games for the demonstration phase,' pp. 15-16): 3. Look, cover, say, check – independent 4. Snap flashcard game – 2–6 players 5. Pairs flashcard game – 2+ players 6. Turn-over – independent 7. Bingo – 2–4 players
Consolidation (revise, apply & reflect)	The consolidation phase is a chance to revise, reflect on their learning and to relate the learning to the learners' own lives by applying it to real life experiences. **Revise:** Write two words (using the learnt vocabulary). However, create a couple of spelling errors. Ask the learners to correct them. Remove them from the board. Ask learners to write the words themselves. Learners should work in pairs to review each other's words. Share one with the group and reflect together. **Apply:** Ask the learners if they know other words like this, e.g. for words associated with food like grapes, oranges (they could take a look at their lunch box or some pictures of associated words in a picture dictionary).' **Reflect:** Following this, they should reflect on their achievement. Did they learn the vocabulary? What additional useful language did they need? (see assessment for learning) Use the Assessment for Learning form in Appendix 3 to identify successes and areas of development. This assessment should inform future learning (revisit this during review sessions). Learners can write down or stick the new learning in their Remember Book (see page 6) to revise at home and in future lessons.

Source: Adapted from Learning Village in Action, 2018

Option B: Language structure lesson (learning sentences or phrases, e.g. There is a mouse.)

Prepare the flashcard resources and sample sentence before you start the lesson.

Session breakdown	Explanation
Review – Use of flashcard resources from previous lessons	This is a review of a previous session. The teacher or learner can plan for this by using the vocabulary/language structure learning games from previous sections, e.g., a snap flashcard game practicing can/can't. (also see Collaborative games for the demonstrate phase, pp. 15-16)
Connection (orientate & assess) – Use of flashcard resources for a new lesson	The connection phase allows the learners to orientate themselves with the context. **Orientate:** Choose 1-2 language structure lesson flashcards (without the text). Ask: 'What can you tell me about these pictures?' Learners can answer in English or in their home language. **Assess:** This also allows both learners and teachers to collaboratively assess understanding and make judgments on what learners need to know: Do they understand the picture? Can they say it in their home language? Can they say it in English?
Activation (explore & recall)	The activation phase is for generating ideas on how you use the pictured language and having a go at using it. **Explore the images** (to support comprehension): Learners look at the Language structure Lesson flashcard resources (shown without text). Ask the learners to guess at orally constructing the sentences for each of the Language Structure Lesson flashcard images (they may know some of the vocabulary as they will have learnt it in the previous lessons). If learners need further help, match the image to the sentence together. However, encourage the learners to try themselves first.
	Explore the sentence (to support construction): Using the cut out the sample sentence above the Language Structure lesson flashcard resources (Chapter 3). Mix up the words and place them face up. Learners should guess how to reconstruct the sentence. If they need help, construct it together. **Consider the grammar:** If there is a grammar learning point, e.g. have/has, ask when they use have and has. If they need help, give clues or a couple of examples to help them understand. Provide the rule and offer further examples for them to apply it. **Recall** (to support memorizing): Say the corresponding sentence for each flashcard. Ask the learners to repeat it. Remove the text from one flashcard and ask the learners to recall it. Then repeat them all together again. Remove the text from a second flashcard and ask the learners to recall both those flashcards without text then repeat them all together again. Continue until the learners are confident in saying all the vocabulary without the text prompts.
Demonstration (refine)	**Show they know the target language:** Help the learners to recall the vocabulary or language structures by providing a method of learning (learners can choose their most effective learning method once they know the games): Choose one of the methods of learning (see 'Collaborative games for the demonstration phase,' pp. 15-16): 3. Look, cover, say, check – independent 4. Snap flashcard game – 2–6 players 5. Pairs flashcard game – 2+ players 6. Turn-over – independent 7. Bingo – 2–4 players

Session breakdown	Explanation
Consolidation (revise, apply & reflect)	The consolidation phase is a chance to revise, reflect on their learning and to relate the learning to the learners' own lives by applying it to real life experiences. **Revise:** Write a sentence (using the learnt language structure) that can be used in their day-to-day life, e.g. 'Do you like bananas?' 'Yes, I do'. However, create a couple of errors, e.g. a spelling error or a missing bit of punctuation, an incorrect word or an incorrect word order. Ask the learners to correct it. Remove it from the board. Ask learners to write the sentence themselves. Learners should work in pairs to review each other's sentence. Share one with the group and reflect together.
	Apply: Ask the learners for other ways to apply the sentence, for example, if they learnt, 'Can you play football?' They might then use 'can' in other contexts, e.g.' Can I have lunch?' Or 'Can I read my book?' **Reflect:** Following this, they should reflect on their achievement. Did they learn the language structure? What additional useful language did they need? (see assessment for learning) Use the Assessment for Learning form in Appendix 3 to identify successes and areas of development. This assessment should inform future learning (revisit this during review sessions). Learners can write down or stick the new learning in their Remember Book (see page 6) to revise at home and in future lessons.

Collaborative games for the demonstration phase

Snap (2-6 players) How to play: 1. Cut out 4 sets of the lesson flashcards (with or without text depending on the needs of the learners), mix them up and deal out an equal number face down in front of each player, until all the cards are distributed. 2. Each learner takes turns to take a card from their pile and put it face-up on a pile in the middle. As they put their card down in the pile, they say the corresponding vocabulary or language structure. 3. If the player turns over a card that matches the previous one, they win all the cards in the pile then the next player starts step 2 again. If the player turns over a card that doesn't match, the next player has a turn. 4. The winner is the learner with the most cards left in their hand.	Pairs (2+ players) How to play: 1. Cut out 2 sets of lesson flashcards (with or without text depending on the needs of the learners), mix them and put them all face down spread out over the table. 2. The first player selects any flashcard, turns it over and says the corresponding vocabulary or language structures. They do the same with another flashcard. If the flashcards match they can keep them. Note that they cannot turn over more than two cards in one go. 3. The next player has a go and does the same, choosing 2 flashcards and saying the corresponding vocabulary or language structures. Players take turns to have a go. 4. The player with the most pairs (after all the flashcards have been collected or after a certain time period) wins.
Bingo (2-4 players) How to play: 1. Cut out 4 sets of lesson flashcards (with or without text depending on the needs of the learners), mix them and put them face down in a pile. 2. Ask each player to pick 6 different lesson flashcards and place them face up in front of them. 3. The teacher calls a vocabulary or language structure text from the flashcard lesson and, if a learner has the corresponding flashcard, they turn it over.	Turn Over (1 player) How to play: 1. Cut out 4 sets of lesson flashcards (with or without text depending on the needs of the learners), mix them up and place them face down in a pile in front of player A. 2. Player A turns one card over at a time and says the corresponding vocabulary or language structure text. If they are correct, they put it in a 'correct' pile.

4. The teacher calls the next vocabulary or language structure text and again, learners with that vocabulary or language structure text turn it over. 5. The teacher continues until a player has turned over all their cards. 6. The first player to turn all their cards over or have the most turned over after a given time is the winner.	3. If they are incorrect, they put it in an 'incorrect' pile. 4. Once the player has finished their pile, they must revisit the incorrect cards and repeat steps 2 and 3., until they get all the cards correct.

Fish (3-5 players)

How to play:

1. Cut out 3 sets of lesson flashcards (without text), mix them up and divide all of the cards between players.
2. Without showing the other players, each player pulls out any group of 3 of the same lesson flashcards. The learner should state the vocabulary or language structure that the flashcard corresponds to. These should then be kept to the side in the 'winning' pile, and they will not be used again.
   - Player A choses a player and asks them for one of their flashcards (the players must hide their cards so player A is guessing that they hold that card in their hand). They must use target language for this, e.g. 'Have you got . . .' 'or 'Do you have . . .' or 'Is it . . .' or 'Would you like . . .' or just the vocabulary words.
   - Player B responds positively if they have the card, e.g. 'Yes, I have.' or 'Yes, it is.' or 'Yes, I would.' and gives player A the card. If this results in player A collecting a set of 3 of the same cards then they must place that set of three in their winning pile and it's the next player's turn. Player B responds negatively if they do not have the card, e.g. 'No, I haven't.' or 'No, it isn't.' or 'No, I wouldn't.' and gives player A nothing and it is the next player's turn.
   - The next player then has a turn to ask another player if they have a card, using the target vocabulary or language structure. Players continue to take turns until all the cards are finished or after a certain time period.
   - The aim of the game is to win the most sets of 3 cards.

Creating a successful lesson

Mother tongue

Using a mother tongue is an essential part of learning a new language. Imagine yourself plunged into a new country with limited grasp of the language spoken. You have such a good grasp over your own language that you would naturally translate. What if someone told you that you shouldn't translate? How would that make you feel? What effect would that have on your learning in the short and long term? With that in mind, consider how you can adjust your practice in schools to ensure we support each learner's home language when, as a teacher, we don't often speak their languages.

(Scott, 2016)

We need to encourage learners to use their mother tongue from day-one to support their understand of the new language and the concept presented (even if it's just making a note of new learning in their mother tongue in a book margin to remind themselves). "It ensures that students' cognitive development continues alongside the learning of the new language" (Sears, 2015).

Mother tongue should be widely used throughout the programme; every session starts with an opportunity to 'connect' which is an ideal time for learners to translate. Here are some useful suggestions for making connections with mother tongue in the induction-to-English and their curriculum studies:

- Use translators (Google Translate, translation pens, dictionaries). These days, you can glide the camera of an iPhone or iPad over text to get an instant translation to the language of your choice or, even simpler, speak into the app and your translation can be given in text or audio. If iPhones or iPads aren't an option, translation pens or Google translate on laptops are good alternatives.
- Set homework for learners to discuss topics at home with parents so that the learners get a fuller understanding of the topic and develop the vocabulary in their home language. The role of parents should not be underestimated. Parents need to try to promote academic development of their child's mother tongue at home.
- Pair students by home language so they can discuss the topic in their home language before being asked for responses in English.

- Ask learners to use their Remember Book, which shows vocabulary in both English and their mother tongue. Teach the learners how to use it by looking, covering, saying and checking (see page 6).
- Encourage students to translate new vocabulary and language structures in class and write in the home language in their books to help them remember.
- For fast vocabulary learning, provide learners with flashcards (and useful ways to use them), populated by themselves in English and their home language (perhaps on the back of the images so they can hide the answers easily).
- Learners can share work completed in their home language with other learners, with parents or with the class in both languages.
- Ask learners to compare specific language structures with their mother tongue and identify the differences. These differences help them to be more aware of how both languages are formed and to use both more accurately.

(Adapted from Scott, 2016)

Effective planning

The teacher of the programme should be responsible for the planning. Some planning time will be required at the beginning of every week in order to look at each learner's needs from their baseline assessment and Assessment for Learning form. This can be used to consider the bespoke needs of the learners and to resource the programme. Revision sections should be included in the planning in order to revisit the vocabulary and language structures that learners found challenging or focus on useful vocabulary that arose when teaching.

Patience

Learners need time to think. Do not be tempted to answer for them. If you can see they can't answer, maybe a prompt would help them remember half of what they are learning. Remembering half is better than giving them the whole new learning again. Obviously, do not labour a point. If they really don't understand, just be positive and give them the answer. Maybe you could say, 'We don't know that. We will do it again later. Have a good look at it so that you know next time.' Then come back to it at the end of the lesson.

Success and praise

With regards to praise and encouragement, Clarke (2001) outlined that, "the language of praise can have varying effects on children's self-esteem and ability to be self-evaluative and independent." She outlined the importance of praise appropriate to a learning culture. "Praise is like other forms of reward which discourage children from judging for themselves what is right and wrong. Praise may lead to dependency because children come to rely on the authority figure to tell them what is right or wrong, good or bad" (Kamii, 1984, quoted in Clarke, 2001). Clarke identifies research by Highscope (1995, quoted in Clarke, 2001) which suggests rewards can be related to the learning culture by acknowledging learners' work with specific comments; for example, 'I notice you used a capital letter correctly, that's the first time I have seen you do this. It shows you understand how to use a capital letter.' Comments like these are far more effective than saying, 'Well done' with no reference to what was achieved. Another form of good practice is to "encourage children to describe their efforts, ideas and products by asking open ending questions – 'What can you tell me about . . .?,' 'How did you . . .?,' 'I notice you've . . .,' 'What will you do next?' This gives them power to become self-evaluative." (Clarke, 2001)

Remember, it is also important for learners to be successful, even if this means going slower or recapping again. If they are not successful, they will not be achieving, probably not be motivated and therefore not be keen to learn. Positive encouragements need to be used at every appropriate opportunity.

Use words such as:

- 'Try again.'
- 'You made a mistake, great, we can learn from this.'
- 'Good effort, have you looked at doing it this way?'
- 'If you can do . . . you're doing really well.' (Only say this if you know they can.)

Try to be specific with your praise by using words such as:

- 'I like the way you . . .'
- 'You made the mistake of . . . we can learn from this.'

If you want learners to correct themselves, try not to use a negative comment. Instead, say: 'Try that again. Does it sound right?' If they can't say it, model it for them and then get them to do it. Model it again if they still can't do it. Do this until they CAN do it! Remember, they should be successful.

Avoid negativity. Stay away from words such as:

- 'No.'
- 'Wrong.'
- 'You didn't do this.'
- 'You forgot the . . .'

Total physical response

Total physical response allows language learners to present the meaning of what they hear by using their bodies rather than requiring them to speak. A recent study looked at the effectiveness of learners performing motions with their bodies to express their understanding of what they heard (Hwang et al, 2014). The results showed that this method resulted in internalization of the English language learning and promoted long-term retention, increasing the likelihood that learners will be able to apply what they have learned to daily life. The use of actions to support learning can make an impact.

Phonics

Phonics and reading can be included in small-group support:

The Rose report (2006) identifies the 'importance of phonics as the prime approach to teaching word recognition for the vast majority of children, including those with EAL'. Additionally, current evidence strongly indicates a critical role for "phonological processing (and in particular phonological awareness) and letter-sound knowledge in the development of word-decoding skills in both L1 and L2 reading development" (Genesee et al., 2013).

Learners' home language may not have the same alphabet or offer the same corresponding phonemes (e.g. much 'm-u-ch' sounded in English may not be read quite the same in German and vice versa). Assess the new learners in phonics and then teach to their needs. It's unlikely they will need to spend the same amount of time on phonics as a younger learner who is learning to be literate for the first time. Learners need short quick sessions that focus on progress. For ages 7–9, there is usually access to a phonics revision programme within schools. However, for ages 9–11, phonics is not usually provided as, in most circumstances, fluent learners have acquired the skills. There is usually a person responsible for phonics in every school (in a Learning Support department in a Secondary setting) to seek advice if provision is not in place.

Non-literate learners

Some learners may not be literate in their home language, so reading and writing for the first time in English will be challenging. If learners have not mastered the basics of phonics and aren't yet reading, it is still important we provide an induction-to-English so they can learn words and phrases to help them access the world around them. Phonics should not replace the induction-to-English. Induction-to-English can still be provided if learners aren't literate. They will require additional phonics support during a lesson by using initial letter sounds to match words to images. This supports the learner with the first steps in associating sounds with text. Remember that learners have the right to access the language whether they are literate or not. The induction-to-English can be learnt entirely through speaking and listening activities related to the meaningful images included in the programme. This speaking and listening induction can be delivered alongside phonics.

Reading

This programme does not incorporate a guided reading session. It is advised that a teacher provides beginners to English with daily-guided reading opportunities. Guided readers that are high interest yet at a suitable age level for absolute beginners are hard to source. However, it is possible to buy guided readers specifically geared towards learners learning English (EAL-guided readers contain a limited number of carefully selected words written in basic tenses). There are also comprehension questions in the back of most of these books that would be helpful for the learners to complete with some support. Although not designed exactly for EAL learners, 'catch-up' guided readers which teach phonics can also be useful as they offer books aimed at slightly older learners and can offer a chance to integrate phonics teaching (an area often under-serviced for older learners who may still need this support) (e.g. www. phonicbooks.co.uk).

EAL learners, like any other learner, require good reading models. There may be opportunities for the EAL learners to listen to a class reading-book that may be considerably more difficult than their reading ability. In cases like this, if you have an additional adult in the class, consider reading basic stories to your EAL learners with patterns and rhythm of language. Here's a starting framework for your sessions (sessions can be daily – don't be afraid to repeat):

1   Read the book slowly, introducing vocabulary.
2   Read the book and ask the names of new vocabulary.
3   Read the book and ask the learner to read small, familiar parts with you.
4   and 5 You read, they read or read together

3
The programme

The programme overview

Pre-induction sessions

	Pre-induction sessions	Example
A	Clarifying things	I don't know.
B	Feelings	I am thirsty.
C	School subjects	Science
D	Rooms in the school	Classroom
E	Can I...?	Can I go to the toilet please?
F	Classroom instructions	Write your name on it.

Induction session contents

No.	Session name	Vocabulary learning challenge	Language structures (or grammatical) learning challenge	Ideas for cross-curricular links
1	Making friends	Introductory vocabulary	What's your name? My name is... How are you? She is...	Personal social education – meeting people
2	Counting 1–20	Numbers 1–20	How old are you? I am . . . years old.	Maths – numbers
3	Colours & the classroom	Colours Classroom vocabulary	Is it...? Yes, it is./No, it isn't.	Science – light (colours) Geography – facts about a place
4	Classroom vocabulary & a/an	Classroom instructions – in book? Vowels	a/an	Art – observational drawing (classroom objects)
5	What's that in English?		What's this/that? It's a/an...	History – identifying artefacts

19

No.	Session name	Vocabulary learning challenge	Language structures (or grammatical) learning challenge	Ideas for cross-curricular links
6	His, hers, yours, my	Possessive adjectives: His, hers, yours, my	Whose is this/that? It's...	PE – identifying kit Personal social education – looking after property
7	Numbers 20–50	Numbers Add, subtract, times, divide		Maths – numbers, calculations
8	Likes and dislikes	Levels of like Subject vocabulary	I like . . . I don't like. . .	Maths – tally charts Art – stating preferences
9	Subject + verb + object	Verbs	Pronoun plus verb Word order	Literacy – writing about a character's daily routine (add 'and then' and 'also')
10	Animals and plurals	Animal vocabulary	This is a/an. . . (Irregular) plurals	Science – identifying types of animals, e.g. omnivore, carnivore
11	This, that, these, those		What are these? These are. . .	PE – identifying equipment
12	Imperatives		Imperatives	Literacy – writing instructions
13	Immediate family & have got/has/got	Family vocabulary	How many brothers and sisters has he/she got? He/she has got. . .	Art – portraits Geography – study of families in different cultures
14	Extended family & possessives	Family vocabulary	Who is this? This is. . .	Geography – family trees
15	Description & had got/ have got	Descriptions/attributes vocabulary	He has got. . .	Literacy – describing characters Geography – describing people
16	Sports & Do you like . . . Yes, I do/No, I don't	Sports vocabulary	Do you like. . . ? Yes, I do./No, I don't.	PE – naming sports Literacy – talking about likes and dislikes
17	Can/can't for ability	Sports vocabulary	He can. . .	PE – types of sport

No.	Session name	Vocabulary learning challenge	Language structures (or grammatical) learning challenge	Ideas for cross-curricular links
18	Ordinal numbers	Ordinals 1st – 10th		Maths – numbers, ordinals Science – ordering experiment results Music – counting beats
19	Hobbies	Hobbies vocabulary		History – hobbies in the past
20	Have you got. . . ?	Food vocabulary	Do you have. . . ? Yes, I have got. . .	Science – food groups Science – making healthy food choices
21	Classifiers		I have/haven't got a/an/some	Science – types of packaging Design & technology – designing packaging
22	How much/how many	Food vocabulary	How much/many . . . have you got?	Maths – weighing food Geography – consumer shopping habits
23	Home and there is/are. . .	Rooms of the house vocabulary Home	There is/are. . . There isn't/aren't. . .	Art – observation History – then and now
24	Prepositions		There is/are a/an/some. . .	Art – observation Maths – locating objects
25	Can/can't for permission		Can I. . . ? Yes, you can./No, you can't.	Personal social education –school rules
26	Do you/does he. . . ?	Hobbies	Do you. . .?/Does he. . .? No, I don't./Yes, he does.	Maths – collecting data Literacy – asking questions
27	Would you like. . . ?	Food and drinks vocabulary	What would you like? I would like. . . Would you like. . . ? Yes, I would./No, I wouldn't, thank you.	Geography – food preferences around the world
28	Feelings	Wants and feelings vocabulary	He is. . . She wants to. . .	Personal, social education – feelings
29	Shops and places	Places vocabulary	Where is/are. . . ? It is. . .	Geography – town planning, map reading
30	Directions	Directions vocabulary	Where is. . . ?	Maths – directions

Overview: pre-induction sessions

The learner can use these pictures or statements by showing or pointing to what they need. Set aside some time before they begin class to work with a buddy, parents, mentor, teaching assistant or teacher to learn how to use them. Learners should be encouraged to translate the flashcards. Buddies or parents can assist.

Pre-induction language flashcards

These flashcards can be placed on a learner's desk to assist with communication.

A. Clarifying things

1. Say that again please.	2. I don't understand.
3. In my language this is...	4. What's this in English?
5. Is this right?	

22

© Caroline Scott (2020), *An English as an Additional Language (EAL) Programme: Learning Through Images for 7–14-Year-Olds*, Routledge

B. Feelings

I am hot/cold.	I am hungry/thirsty.
I am happy/sad.	I am upset.
I am unwell.	

23

C. School Subjects

These flashcards can be used to create a visual timetable.

1. Lunchtime	2. Break time
3. English	4. Maths
5. Art	6. Geography
7. Physical Education	8. Religious Education
9. Information Technology	10. Science
13. Reading	14. History

D. Rooms in a school

These flashcards can be placed collaboratively on rooms in the school.

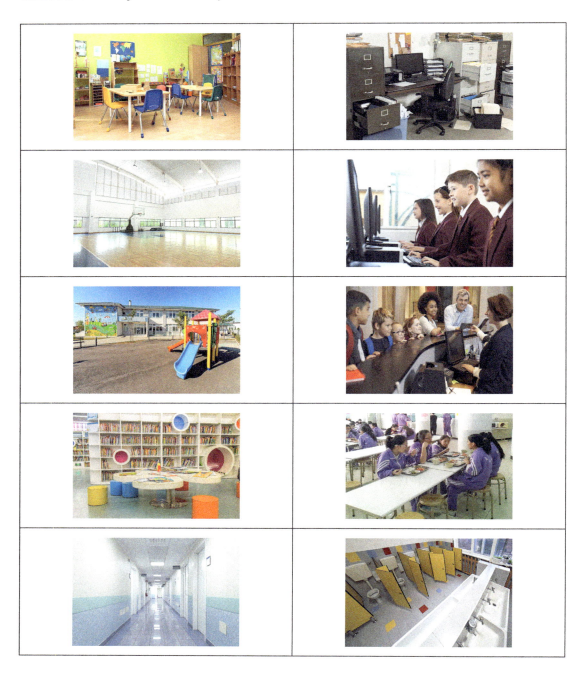

1. A classroom	2. An office
3. A hall	4. An ICT suite
5. A playground	6. The reception
7. A library	8. A canteen
9. A corridor	10. The toilets

E. Can I . . . ?

Flashcards can be made into a key ring and used as a communication tool.

1. Can you write your name, please?	2. Can I have that, please?
3. Can you take me to my classroom, please?	4. Can I go to the toilet, please?
5. Can you help me, please?	6. Can I borrow your pen, please?
7. Can I play, please?	8. Can we be friends, please?

© Caroline Scott (2020), *An English as an Additional Language (EAL) Programme: Learning Through Images for 7–14-Year-Olds*, Routledge

F. Classroom instructions

A great game to start a friendship – buddies and new arrivals can create actions for each flashcard, then buddies can say the instruction and the new arrival mimes it.

1. Be quiet.	2. Listen.
3. Talk to your partner.	4. Read your book.
5. Work on the computer.	6. Go to lunch.
7. Put your hand up.	8. Hand in your homework.
9. Stand up.	10. Sit down.

Induction session details and resources

Please refer back to Chapter 2 ('Cycle of teacher-supported learning') on how to deliver a lesson using these resources. If no resources are included, notes are available on resources to use to support the learning. Be aware that sometimes, there are no sentence reconstructions when the lesson doesn't lend itself to a structured pattern or is a vocabulary lesson. Lessons are labelled vocabulary lesson or language structures lesson, which follow option A or B in the lesson details in the cycle of teacher-supported learning.

Fix the Learning Journey Resource Sheet (below) to the wall and mark off the learners' learning journey location as they progress through the induction. This will support them further in taking more ownership of their learning (they can see what they have learnt and what they are learning next). You could copy the page and mark off the ones you have done if you end up delivering the programme out of order. Encourage them to try and learn themselves before your lesson occurs (if you use the sister programme [www.learningvillage.net], there are additional resources for this).

© Caroline Scott (2020), *An English as an Additional Language (EAL) Programme: Learning Through Images for 7–14-Year-Olds*, Routledge

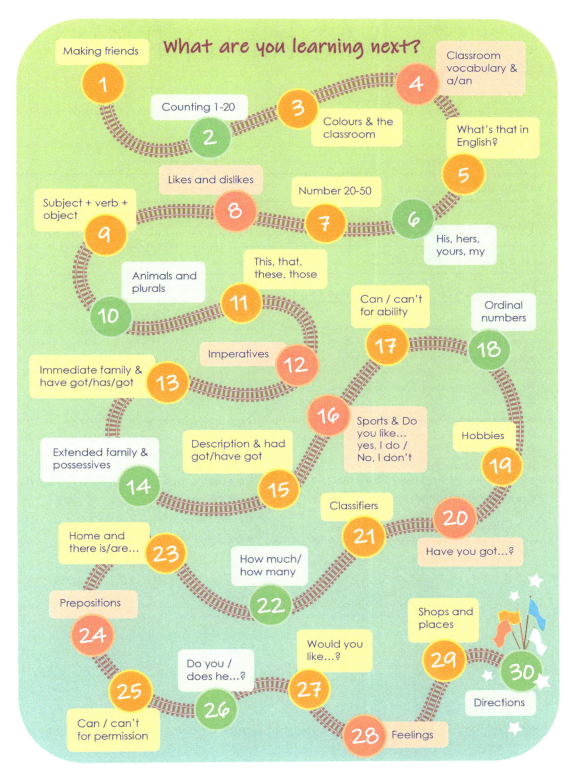

Figure 3.1 Learning journey resource sheet

© Caroline Scott (2020), *An English as an Additional Language (EAL) Programme: Learning Through Images for 7–14-Year-Olds*, Routledge

Making friends

Vocabulary and language structures

Lesson A: Greetings

What's your name? My name is...	What's its name? Its name is...
What's his name? His name is...	What's her name? Her name is...

Lesson B: How are you?

How are you? I am fine, thanks.	How is he? He is fine.
How is she? She is fine.	How are they? They are fine.
How is _____? _____ is fine.	How is it? It is fine.

Also advised:

- Where do you come from? I come from...
- Yes/No
- Spelling their name
- Full stop
- Question mark
- Good morning, hello

Grammar rule 'to be':

Grammar rule: is/am/are (the verb 'to be')
How are you? I am fine, thanks.
How is she? She is fine.

How are they? They are fine.
How is he? He is fine.
How is Tom? He is fine.

Description:

We use is/am/are (to be) to talk about experiencing heat, cold, hunger, thirst or some other common physical condition; we normally use 'be' or 'feel' plus an adjective.

We also use it to talk about weight, size, shape, age, height, length and colour.

Lesson Resources 1a, language structure lesson: Greetings

Cut out the following sentence ready for reconstruction.

What's	your	name	?	My
name	is	Jana	.	

1. What's your name?
   My name is Jana.

2. What's its name?
   Its name is Bo.

3. What's his name?
   His name is Kim.

4. What's her name?
   Her name is Miya.

© Caroline Scott (2020), *An English as an Additional Language (EAL) Programme: Learning Through Images for 7–14-Year-Olds*, Routledge

SESSION 1

Lesson Resources 1b, language structure lesson: How are you?

Cut out the following sentence ready for reconstruction.

How	are	you	?	I
am	fine	,	thanks	.

1. How are you? I am fine, thanks.	2. How is he? He is fine.
3. How is she? She is fine.	4. How are they? They are fine.
5. How is Tom? Tom is fine.	6. How is it? It is fine.

© Caroline Scott (2020), *An English as an Additional Language (EAL) Programme: Learning Through Images for 7–14-Year-Olds*, Routledge

Counting 1-20

SESSION 2

Vocabulary and language structures

Lesson A: Counting 1–10

Use pencils or counters

Lesson B: Counting 1–20

Use pencils or counters

Lesson C: How old are you?

How old are you? I am __ years old.	How old is he? He is __ years old.
How is she? She is fine.	How are they? They are fine.
How is _____? _____ is fine.	How is it? It is fine.

Also advised:

- ▨ Reading and writing numbers 1–10
- ▨ Reading and writing numbers 11–20

Grammar rule 'to be':

Grammar rule: is/am/are (the verb 'to be')
How are you? I am fine, thanks.
How is she? She is fine.
How are they? They are fine.

How is he? He is fine.
How is Tom? He is fine.

Description:

We use is/am/are (to be) to talk about experiencing heat, cold, hunger, thirst or some other common physical condition. We normally use 'be' or 'feel' plus an adjective.

We also use it to talk about weight, size, shape, age, height, length and colour.

35

Lesson Resources 2c language structure lesson: How old are you?

Cut out the following sentence ready for reconstruction.

How	old	are	you	?
I	am	18	years	old

1. How old are you? I am 18 years old.	2. How old is he? He is 6 years old.
3. How old is she? She is 9 years old.	4. How old are they? They are 1 year old.
5. How old is Mina? Mina is 5 years old.	6. How old is it? It is 3 years old.

Colours and the classroom

SESSION 3

Vocabulary and language structures

Lesson A: Colours

Use coloured pencils

Lesson B: Classroom vocabulary

pen	pencil
paper	rubber
reading book	scissors
window	door
exercise book	table
whiteboard	chair

Lesson C: Is it. . . ? Yes, it is./No, it isn't.

Is it blue? No, it isn't.	Is it white? Yes, it is.
Is it black? No, it isn't.	Is it orange? Yes, it is.

Also advised

- Additional classroom vocabulary relevant to your classroom, e.g. literacy book, maths book, school bag, drawing paper, choosing time area.
- A variety of colours, e.g. red, blue, yellow, purple, cream, white.
- Is it. . . (name classroom item)? Yes, it is./No, it isn't.

Grammar rule: Question tags using 'be' (present tense form of 'to be')

- To ask a question, you usually use be, do, have (auxiliary verbs) or can, will, may (example modal verbs). If you want a yes/no answer, then the question starts with the auxiliary or modal verb.
- The word 'is' is used to talk about a person or thing (1 = singular).
- The word 'are' is used to talk about a person or thing (2+ = plural).

37

SESSION 3

Lesson Resources 3b, vocabulary lesson: Classroom vocabulary

1. pen	2. pencil
3. paper	4. rubber
5. reading book	6. scissors

© Caroline Scott (2020), *An English as an Additional Language (EAL) Programme: Learning Through Images for 7–14-Year-Olds*, Routledge

SESSION 3

7. window	8. door
9. notebook	10. table
11. whiteboard	12. chair

Lesson Resources 3c, language structure lesson: Is it. . . ? Yes, it is./No, it isn't.

Cut out the following sentence ready for reconstruction.

Is	it	blue	?	No
,	it	isn't		.

1. Is it blue? No, it isn't.	2. Is it white? Yes, it is.
3. Is it brown? Yes, it is.	4. Is it silver? Yes, it is.
5. Is it red? No, it isn't.	6. Is it orange? No, it isn't.

© Caroline Scott (2020), *An English as an Additional Language (EAL) Programme: Learning Through Images for 7–14-Year-Olds*, Routledge

Classroom vocabulary and a/an

SESSION 4

Vocabulary and language structures

Lesson A: Vowel sounds

Write the vowels a, e, i, o, u on the board.

Lesson B: A/an

A book	An orange pen
A classroom	An egg
An ant	An apple
A tree	A toilet

Lesson C: Classroom instructions – in book?

A tick	A cross
An arrow	Circle the answer
Put a circle around it	Underline it

Also advised:

- a/an with classroom vocabulary
- Speaking and listening marking activity – you say, they do, e.g. write your name, underline your name, write the date, write number 1–3 underneath, circle number 2, etc.
- Feedback on marking in books – what do all the marks mean?

Grammar rule: a/an (article)

We use 'an' before singular (i.e. not plural) nouns that start with a vowel sound (a, e, i, o, u), e.g. an elephant.

We use 'a' before singular nouns that do not start with a vowel sound, e.g. a banana.

41

SESSION 4

Lesson Resources 4b, vocabulary lesson: a/an (consider the grammar point when teaching this lesson)

1. a book	2. an orange pen
3. a classroom	4. an egg

5. an ant	6. an apple
7. a tree	8. a toilet

SESSION 4

Lesson Resources 4c, vocabulary lesson: Classroom instructions – in book?

✓	✗
←	Learning is <u>fun</u>!
YES (NO)	[image of girl writing in book]

1. a tick	2. a cross
3. an arrow	4. Underline it.
5. Circle the answer.	6. Write it down.

What's that in English?

SESSION 5

Vocabulary and language structures

Lesson A: This and that

What's this in English? I don't know.	What's this? It's a computer.
What's that in English? It's an. . .	What's this? It's a toothbrush.
What's this in English? It's a. . .	What's this? It's a whiteboard.

Also advised:

- Pairs game – One person in the pair points to items in the room and the other identifies it (if they can) or says, 'I don't know.'

Grammar rule: What's this/that? It's a/an . . .

- 'What's this?' is the same as saying 'What is this?'

- We use 'What is this?' for a singular noun that is near, e.g. 'You can have this pencil' (said as you give the pencil to a person).
- 'What's that?' is the same as saying 'What is that?'
- We use 'What is that?' for a singular noun that is further away, e.g. 'You can have that book' (said as you point to a book on the shelf on the other side of the room).
- 'It's. . .' is the same as saying 'It is. . .'.

45

SESSION 5

Lesson Resources 5a, language structure lesson: This and that

Cut out the following sentence ready for reconstruction.

What's	that	in	English	?
I	don't	know	.	

1. What's that in English? I don't know.	2. What's this? It's a computer.
3. What's that in English? It's a bird.	4. What's this? It's a toothbrush.
5. What's this in English? It's a blackboard.	6. What's this? It's a whiteboard.

© Caroline Scott (2020), *An English as an Additional Language (EAL) Programme: Learning Through Images for 7–14-Year-Olds*, Routledge

His, hers, yours, my

SESSION 6

Vocabulary and language structures

Lesson A: Possessive adjectives

his	her
your	my
our	their

Lesson B: Whose is this?

Whose is this? It's my bag.	Whose is this? It's her bag.
Whose is this? It's his bag.	Whose is this? It's your bag.
Whose is this? It's our bag.	Whose is this? It's their bag.

Also advised:

- Identify each other's things.

Grammar rule: Possessive adjectives

- We use possessive adjectives, e.g. your, my, her, his, to say who the noun belongs to. They are placed before the noun, e.g. your pen.

47

SESSION 6

Lesson Resources 6a, vocabulary lesson: Possessive adjectives

1. his	2. her
3. your	4. my
5. our	6. their

© Caroline Scott (2020), *An English as an Additional Language (EAL) Programme: Learning Through Images for 7–14-Year-Olds*, Routledge

Lesson Resources 6a, language structure lesson: Whose is this?

Cut out the following sentence ready for reconstruction.

Whose	is	this	?	It's
my	bag	.		

1. Whose is this? It's my bag.	2. Whose is this? It's her bag.
3. Whose is this? It's his bag.	4. Whose is this? It's your bag.
5. Whose is this? It's our bag.	6. Whose is this? It's their bag.

© Caroline Scott (2020), *An English as an Additional Language (EAL) Programme:*
Learning Through Images for 7–14-Year-Olds, Routledge

Numbers 20-50

SESSION 7

Note that there are good resources available in your classroom to support this lesson; therefore, there are no printable resources included.

Vocabulary and language structures

Lesson A: Counting 20–39

Vocabulary lesson – Use pencils or counters to learn to count. Start by teaching up to 5, then 10, then 15, etc. Focus on repetition and confidence before moving onto higher numbers.

Lesson B: Calculation

Vocabulary lesson – Write the symbol for add, subtract, multiply, divide on self-made flashcards.

Also advised:

- Teach the words plus, take away, times, shared and equals.
- Teach how to add.
- Teach how to subtract.
- Teach how to multiply.
- Teach how to divide.

Likes and dislikes

SESSION 8

Vocabulary and language structures

Lesson A: Levels of like

I love...	I don't like...
I really like...	I really don't like...
I like...	I hate...
It's ok.	

Lesson B: Subjects

I like reading.	I don't like Geography.
I really like Art.	I really don't like Maths.
I love Science.	I hate reading.

Also advised:

- Talk about other preferences, e.g. colours or maybe even numbers.

Grammar rule: Question tags

- To ask a question, you usually use be, do, have (auxiliary verbs) or can, will, may (example modal verbs). If you want a yes/no answer, then the question starts with the auxiliary or modal verb.

Lesson Resources 8A, language structure lesson: Do you like. . . ?

Cut out the following sentence ready for reconstruction.

I	like	reading	.

I love . . .
I really like. . .
It's ok.
I don't like. . .
I really don't like. . .
I hate.

© Caroline Scott (2020), *An English as an Additional Language (EAL) Programme:*
Learning Through Images for 7–14-Year-Olds, Routledge

51

Lesson Resources 8B, language structure lesson: Do you like...?

1. I like reading.	2. I really like Art.
3. I love Science.	4. I really don't like Maths.
5. Geography is okay.	6. I hate reading.

Subject + verb + object

SESSION 9

Vocabulary and language structures

Lesson A: Verbs

walk	sleep
stand	listen
run	play

Lesson B: Pronoun plus verb

She walks home.	It sleeps in a bed.
I stand here.	He listens to music.
They run in the park.	You play on the computer.

Also advised:

- Personal pronouns
- Act out other relevant basic verbs, e.g. go, come, say, sit, wait, help, tidy.

Grammar rule: Word order

- We can use subject + verb + object to make simple sentences, e.g. Caroline + reads + a book, I + like + cheese.

Grammar rule: Present simple, third person

- Verbs end in 's' or 'es' after he, she, it or a name, e.g. she walks, he walks, it walks, Caroline walks or she watches, he watches, it watches, Caroline watches.
- For most verbs that end in 'o,' 'es' is added, e.g. does, goes.

Lesson Resources 9a, vocabulary lesson: Introduce the basic verbs.

Use the flashcards in 9b to introduce the verbs walk, sleep, stand, listen, run, play without their sentences.

53

SESSION 9

Lesson Resources 9b, language structure lesson: Introduce the verbs in sentences.

Cut out the following sentence ready for reconstruction.

| She | walks | home | . |

1. She walks home.	2. It sleeps in a bed.
3. I stand here.	4. He listens to music.
5. They run in the park.	6. You play on the computer.

54

© Caroline Scott (2020), *An English as an Additional Language (EAL) Programme: Learning Through Images for 7–14-Year-Olds*, Routledge

Animals and plurals

SESSION 10

Vocabulary and language structures

Lesson A: Animals

This is a dog.	This is a cat.
This is a fox.	This is a horse.
This is a wolf.	This is a fish.

Lesson B: Irregular plurals

mouse = mice	foot = feet
sheep = sheep	
man = men	tooth = teeth
woman = women	child = children

Also advised:

- Teach plurals with animals, e.g. 3 foxes, 5 sheep, 6 cows (follow the grammar rule).
- Identify other groups of objects and apply the grammar rule below.

Grammar rule: plurals s/es/ies/ves

- Plural means more than one. When we talk about more than one noun, we usually add an 's,' e.g. chairs.
- When we use nouns ending in 'ch,' 'sh,' 's,' 'x' and 'es,' we add 'es,' e.g. buses, foxes, watches.
- When we use nouns ending in 'y,' e.g. family, we take away the 'y' and add 'ies,' e.g. families.
- When we use nouns ending in 'f' or 'fe,' e.g. wolf, we take away the 'f' or 'fe' and add 'ves,' e.g. wolves.
- Sometimes the word changes or stays the same when we talk about the plural, e.g. children, people, fish, sheep.

55

SESSION 10

Lesson Resources 10a, vocabulary lesson: **Animals**

1. mouse	2. cat
3. fox	4. horse
5. wolf	6. fish

© Caroline Scott (2020), *An English as an Additional Language (EAL) Programme: Learning Through Images for 7–14-Year-Olds*, Routledge

Lesson Resources 10b, vocabulary lesson: Irregular plurals

Refer to the grammar rule for this vocabulary lesson.

1. mouse = mice	2. foot = feet
3. sheep = sheep	4. goose = geese
5. man = men	6. tooth = teeth
7. woman = women	8. child = children

This, that, these, those

SESSION 11

Vocabulary and language structures

Lesson A: This, that, these, those

What are those? Those are boats.	What is this? This is a present.
What is that? That is a wall.	What are these? These are bones.

Also advised:

- Use your school environment to choose objects near and far, plural and singular to bring the lesson to life.

Grammar rule: These/those

- We use 'this' for a singular noun that is near, e.g. 'You can have this apple' (said as you give the apple to the person).

- We use 'that' for a singular noun that is further away, e.g. 'You can have that book' (said as you point to a book on the shelf on the other side of the room).
- We use 'these' to talk about plural nouns that are near, e.g. 'You can have these keys' (said as you give the keys to the person).
- We use 'those' to talk about plural nouns that are further away, e.g. 'You can have those books' (said as you point to the bookshelf on the other side of the room).

Lesson Resources 11a, language structure lesson: This, that, these, those

Cut out the following sentence ready for reconstruction.

What	are	those	?	Those
are	boats	.		

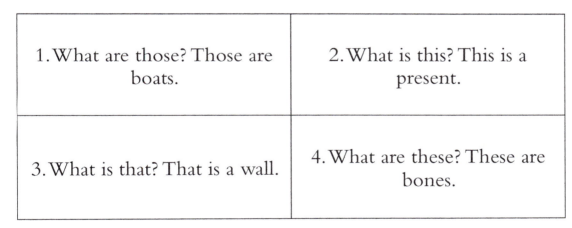

1. What are those? Those are boats.	2. What is this? This is a present.
3. What is that? That is a wall.	4. What are these? These are bones.

© Caroline Scott (2020), *An English as an Additional Language (EAL) Programme: Learning Through Images for 7–14-Year-Olds*, Routledge

Imperatives

SESSION 12

Vocabulary and language structures

Lesson A: Imperatives

Open the door.	Close the door.
Sit down.	Stand up.
Switch off the light.	Switch on the light.

Also advised:

- Learners identify and act out other imperatives.

Grammar rule: Imperatives

- Imperatives, e.g. mind the step, be careful, stand up, don't feed the, don't walk on the, don't take photos, be quiet, don't move quickly, don't eat, no drinks allowed, etc.

Lesson Resources 12a, vocabulary lesson: Imperatives

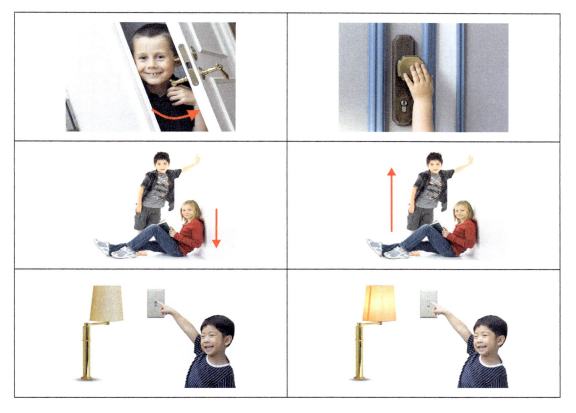

1. Open the door.	2. Close the door.
3. Sit down.	4. Stand up.
5. Switch off the light.	6. Switch on the light.

© Caroline Scott (2020), An English as an Additional Language (EAL) Programme: Learning Through Images for 7–14-Year-Olds, Routledge

SESSION 13

Immediate family and have got/has got

Vocabulary and language structures

Lesson Resources A: Family 1

mum	dad
brother	sister
grandmother	grandfather

Lesson B: Family 2

aunt	uncle
niece	nephew
wife	husband
cousin	baby
son	daughter

Lesson C: How many brothers and sisters have you got?

How many brothers and sisters has she got? She has got...	How many brothers and sisters has he got? He has got...
How many daughters has he got? He has got ... daughters.	How many brothers and sisters have you got?

Also advised:

- Bring in photos of their family.
- Use the term 'How many . . . has she got?' to ask other questions, e.g. How many pencils has she got?

Grammar rule: have/has

- 'Have' is used to talk about relationships, characteristics and possessions as well as similar ideas.
- We use 'have' with I, you, they and we, e.g. I have, you have, they have, we have.
- We use 'has' with she, he, it and a name, e.g. she has, he has, it has, Caroline has.

Lesson Resources A, vocabulary lesson: Family 1

1. mum	2. dad
3. brother	4. sister
5. grandmother	6. grandfather

Lesson Resources B, vocabulary lesson: Family 2

SESSION 13

1. aunt	2. uncle
3. niece	4. nephew
5. wife	6. husband

7. cousin	8. baby
9. son	10. daughter

SESSION 13

Lesson Resources C, language structure lesson: How many brothers and sisters have you got?

Cut out the following sentence ready for reconstruction.

How	many	brothers	and	sisters
has	she	got	?	She
has	got	2	brothers	.

1. How many brothers and sisters has she got? She has got 2 brothers.	2. How many brothers and sisters has he got? He has got one brother and one sister.
3. How many brother and sisters have you got? I have got 1 brother and one sister.	4. How many children have they got? They have got 3 children.
5. How many daughters have they got? They have got 1 daughter.	

© Caroline Scott (2020), *An English as an Additional Language (EAL) Programme: Learning Through Images for 7–14-Year-Olds*, Routledge

Extended family and possessives

SESSION 14

Vocabulary and language structures

Lesson A: Who is this? This is my/her/his . . .

Who is this? This is her mother.	Who is this? This is her father.
Who is this? This is her grandmother.	Who is this? This is his sister.
Who are they? They are my family.	Who is this? This is. . .

Lesson B: Possessive/s

This is Alf's daughter, Pat.	This is Jen's daughter, Pat.
This is Pat's daughter, Maria.	This is Max's daughter, Maria.

Also advised:

- Revise possessive adjectives, e.g. her pencil (Lila's pencil), his pencil (Tim's pencil), my pencil, your pencil.
- Use classroom objects and ask 'Whose _____ (e.g. pencil) is this?' 'It's ___'s pencil.'

Grammar rule: Possessive/s ('s)

- We use − 's to show when something belongs to someone, e.g. Caroline's bag (the bag that belongs to Caroline).

67

Lesson Resources 14A, language structure lesson: Who is this? This is my/her/his...

Cut out the following sentence ready for reconstruction.

| Who | is | this | ? | This |
| is | his | mother | . | |

1. Who is this? This is his mother.	2. Who is this? This is her father.
3. Who is this? This is his grandmother.	4. Who is this? This is my family.
5. Who is this? This is her grandfather.	

Lesson Resources 14B, language structure lesson:

| This | is | Alf | ' | s |
| daughter | , | Pat | . | |

1. This is Alf's daughter, Pat.	2. This is Jen's daughter, Pat.
3. This is Pat's daughter, Maria.	4. This is Max's daughter, Maria.

SESSION 15

Description and had got/have got

Vocabulary and language structures

Lesson A: Description

blond hair	brown hair
short hair	long hair
brown eyes	blue eyes
curly hair	straight hair

Lesson B: Have got/has got descriptions

He has got green eyes.	We have got ginger hair.
She has got straight hair.	The baby has got blue eyes.
She has got black hair.	You have got brown eyes.

Lesson C: Has not got/have not got descriptions

He hasn't got brown eyes.	I haven't got brown hair.
She hasn't got short hair.	They haven't got. . .
We haven't got. . .	You haven't got. . .

Also advised:

- Other physical characteristics of the learners, e.g. hair styles like 'He has got a pony tail.' or 'I have got a fringe.'

Grammar rule: have not (got), haven't (got)

- 'Have' is used to talk about relationships, characteristics and possessions as well as similar ideas.
- We use 'have' with I, you, they and we, e.g. I have, you have, they have, we have.
- We use 'has' with she, he, it and a name, e.g. she has, he has, it has, Caroline has.
- We use 'not' to make statements negative, e.g. have not/has not = haven't/hasn't

70

Lesson Resources 15A, vocabulary lesson: Description

1. blond hair	2. brown hair
3. short hair	4. long hair
5. brown eyes	6. blue eyes
7. curly hair	8. straight hair

© Caroline Scott (2020), *An English as an Additional Language (EAL) Programme: Learning Through Images for 7–14-Year-Olds*, Routledge

SESSION 15

Lesson Resources 15B, language structure lesson: Have got/has got descriptions

Cut out the following sentence ready for reconstruction.

| It | has | got | blue | eyes | . |

1. It has got blue eyes.	2. We have got blond hair.
3. She has got straight hair.	4. The baby has got blue eyes.
5. She has got black hair.	6. I have got brown eyes.

© Caroline Scott (2020), *An English as an Additional Language (EAL) Programme: Learning Through Images for 7–14-Year-Olds*, Routledge

Lesson Resources 15C, language structure lesson: Has not got/have not got descriptions

Cut out the following sentence ready for reconstruction.

He	hasn't	got	brown	eyes
.

1. He hasn't got brown eyes.	2. I haven't got curly hair.
3. She hasn't got short hair.	4. They haven't got brown hair.
5. We haven't got curly hair.	6. You haven't got black hair.

© Caroline Scott (2020), *An English as an Additional Language (EAL) Programme: Learning Through Images for 7–14-Year-Olds*, Routledge

Sports and do you like . . . yes, I do/no, I don't

SESSION 16

Vocabulary and language structures

Lesson A: Sports

basketball	football
tennis	golf
cricket	cycling
baseball	swimming
badminton	table tennis
running	rugby

Lesson B: Do you like. . . ?

Do you like badminton? Yes, I do.	Do they like cycling? Yes, they do.
Does she like football? No, she doesn't.	Does he like swimming? Yes, he does.
Do they like running? Yes, they do.	Does she like tennis? Yes, she does.
Does he like cricket? No, he doesn't.	Does she like golf? No, she doesn't.

Also advised:

- Teach and act out other sports they play but that aren't included.
- Ask if they like other things, like, 'Do you like Maths?' 'Do you like school?'

Grammar rule: Do you/Does he?

- We use 'do' to make questions with verbs, e.g. Do you like football?
- We use 'do' with 'I,' 'you,' 'they,' 'we,' e.g. Do you. . . ?
- We use 'does' with, 'he,' 'she,' 'it,' a name, e.g. Does Caroline like football?

74

Lesson Resources 16A, vocabulary structure lesson: Sports

1. basketball	2. football
3. tennis	4. golf
5. cricket	6. cycling

SESSION 16

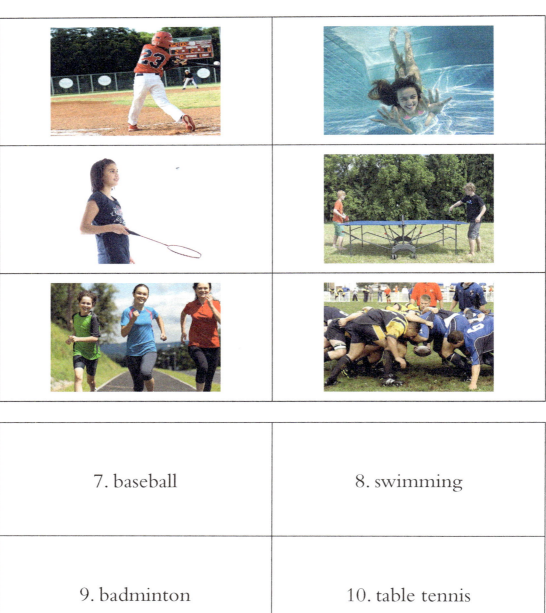

7. baseball	8. swimming
9. badminton	10. table tennis
11. running	12. rugby

Lesson Resources 16B, language structure lesson: Do you like. . .?

Cut out the following sentence ready for reconstruction.

Do	you	like	badminton	?
Yes	I	do	.	

1. Do you like badminton? Yes, I do.	2. Do they like cycling? Yes, they do.
3. Does she like football? No, she doesn't.	4. Does he like swimming? Yes, he does.

SESSION 16

© Caroline Scott (2020), *An English as an Additional Language (EAL) Programme: Learning Through Images for 7–14-Year-Olds*, Routledge

SESSION 16

5. Do they like running? Yes, they do.	6. Does she like tennis? Yes, she does.
7. Does he like cricket? No, he doesn't.	8. Does she like golf? No, she doesn't.

Can/can't for ability

SESSION 17

Vocabulary and language structures

Lesson A: Can/can't and sport

He can play basketball.	She can play football.
They can't surf.	We can't cycle.
I can play tennis.	You can play squash.

Also advised:

- Include other sports and other things they can and can't do.

Grammar rule: can for ability

- We use 'can' to talk about ability, e.g. I can swim.
- We use 'cannot' in the negative form.
- Cannot is often shortened to 'can't' when we write informally or speak.

79

Lesson Resources 17A, language structure lesson: Can/can't and sport

Cut out the following sentence ready for reconstruction.

| He | can | play | basketball | . |

1. He can play basketball.	2. She can't swim.
3. They can't surf.	4. She can't cycle.
5. I can play tennis.	6. She can play squash.

© Caroline Scott (2020), *An English as an Additional Language (EAL) Programme: Learning Through Images for 7–14-Year-Olds*, Routledge

Ordinal numbers

SESSION 18

Vocabulary and language structures

Lesson A, ordinal numbers

first	sixth
second	seventh
third	
fourth	
fifth	

Also advised:

- Use the school leader-boards or sports day results to talk about learner places, e.g. first, second, third.
- Consider teaching eighth, ninth, tenth, eleventh, twelfth.

Lesson A, vocabulary lesson: Ordinal numbers

Use the picture to point out first to seventh place in the race.

first
second
third
fourth
fifth
sixth
seventh

© Caroline Scott (2020), *An English as an Additional Language (EAL) Programme: Learning Through Images for 7–14-Year-Olds*, Routledge

Hobbies

SESSION 19

Vocabulary and language structures

Lesson A: Hobbies

Dancing	Listening to music
Going to the cinema	Reading
Playing on the computer	Playing football
Watching television	

Also advised:

- Learners use picture dictionaries to find more hobbies.

Lesson Resources A, vocabulary lesson: Hobbies

1. Dancing.	2. Listening to music.
3. Going to the cinema.	4. Reading.
5. Playing on the computer.	6. Playing football.
7. Watching television.	

SESSION 20

Have you got. . . ?

Vocabulary and language structures

Lesson A: a, an and some

a hamburger	an apple
some rice	some salad
a banana	some oranges

Lesson B: Have you got any food?

1. Have you got any rice? Yes, I have got some rice.	2. Have you got a hamburger? Yes, I have got a hamburger.
3. Have you got any salad? Yes, I have got some salad.	4. Have you got an egg? Yes, I have got an egg.
5. Have you got a biscuit? No, I haven't got a biscuit.	6. Have you got a biscuit? Yes, I have got a biscuit.

Also advised:

- Use a picture dictionary or the school canteen to learn other foods.

Grammar rule: countable/uncountable nouns

- Countable nouns are the names of things that we can count, e.g. an egg, two tables.
- Uncountable nouns are the names of things we can't count, e.g. sugar, coffee, sand.
- Uncountable nouns do not have a plural form, e.g. 'sugars' is not correct.
- We use uncountable nouns and plurals with 'some,' e.g. some sugar, some eggs.
- We use countable nouns with 'a,' 'an' or 'the,' e.g. an egg, a packet of sugar.

Grammar rule: have you got any. . . ?

- We use 'any' when it doesn't matter which one we are referring to (in this case, we use it with an uncountable noun or plural), e.g. any biscuits, any food, any rice.
- 'Have' is used to talk about relationships, characteristics and possessions as well as similar ideas. Here it is used to talk about possession, e.g. Have you got any clothes?

Lesson Resources A, vocabulary lesson: a, an and some

SESSION 20

85

SESSION 20

Lesson Resources B, language structure lesson: Have you got any food?

Cut out the following sentence ready for reconstruction.

Have	you	got	any	rice
?	Yes	,	I	have
got	some	rice	.	

1. Have you got any rice? Yes, I have got some rice.	2. Have you got a hamburger? Yes, I have got a hamburger.
3. Have you got any salad? Yes, I have got some salad.	4. Have you got an egg? Yes, I have got an egg.

© Caroline Scott (2020), *An English as an Additional Language (EAL) Programme: Learning Through Images for 7–14-Year-Olds*, Routledge

5. Have you got a biscuit? No, I haven't got a biscuit.	6. Have you got a biscuit? Yes, I have got a biscuit.
5. Have you got an orange? No, I haven't got an orange.	6. Have you got an orange? Yes, I have got an orange.

Classifiers

SESSION 21

Vocabulary and language structures

Lesson A: Classifiers

a glass of	a bag of
a cup of	a tin of
a plate of	a piece of
a bottle of	a box of
a can of	a carton of

Lesson B: I have got a/an or some/I haven't

I have got a tin of tuna.	I have got a bottle of water.
I have got an apple.	I have got some ice cream.
I have got a piece of cake.	

Also advised:

- Teach other classifiers with other foods or items, e.g. a packet of crisps.

Grammar rule: Classifying uncountable nouns into units

- We use 'of' with words that refer to units, e.g. piece of paper, packet of crisps.
- We can make uncountable nouns become countable in this form, e.g. we can count a cup of tea but not tea, we can count packets of sugar, but not sugar.

Lesson Resources A, vocabulary lesson: Classifiers

1. a glass of	2. a bag of
3. a cup of	4. a tin of
5. a plate of	6. a piece of

© Caroline Scott (2020), *An English as an Additional Language (EAL) Programme: Learning Through Images for 7–14-Year-Olds*, Routledge

SESSION 21

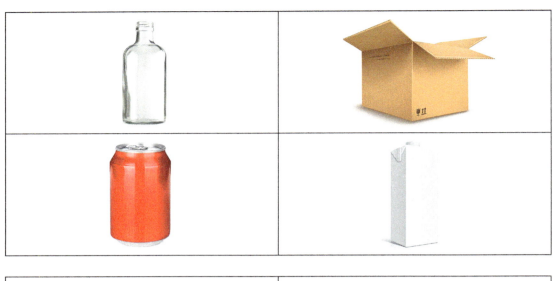

7. a bottle of	8. a box of
9. a can of	10. a carton of

Lesson Resources B, language structure lesson: I have got a/an or some/I haven't

Cut out the following sentence ready for reconstruction.

| I | have | got | a | bottle |
| of | water | . | | |

1. I have got a bottle of water.	2. I have got an apple.
3. I have got some rice.	4. I have got a piece of cake.

© Caroline Scott (2020), *An English as an Additional Language (EAL) Programme: Learning Through Images for 7–14-Year-Olds*, Routledge

SESSION 22

How much/how many . . .

Vocabulary and language structures

Lesson A: Much or many

How many sausages have you got?	How much pasta have you got?
How many biscuits have you got?	How much milk have you got?
How many shrimps have you got?	How much rice have you got?
How much water have you got?	How many potatoes have you got?
How much sugar have you got?	How many eggs have you got?
How much cheese have you got?	How many burgers have you got?

Also advised:

- Other foods that are uncountable.

Grammar rule: Much/many

- 'Much' and 'many' are usually common in questions and negatives, e.g. How many have you got?
- We use 'much' with singular (uncountable) nouns, e.g. How much sugar have you got?
- We use 'many' with plurals, e.g. How many eggs have you got?

Grammar rule: Classifying uncountable nouns into units

- We use 'of' with words that refer to units, e.g. piece of paper, packet of crisps.
- We can make uncountable nouns become countable in this form, e.g. we can count a cup of tea, but not tea, we can count packets of sugar, but not sugar.

Lesson Resources A, language structure lesson: Much or many

Cut out the following sentence ready for reconstruction.

How	many	sausages	have	you
got	?			

1. How many sausages have you got?	2. How much pasta have you got?
3. How many biscuits have you got?	4. How much milk have you got?
5. How many shrimps have you got?	6. How much rice have you got?

© Caroline Scott (2020), *An English as an Additional Language (EAL) Programme: Learning Through Images for 7–14-Year-Olds*, Routledge

SESSION 22

7. How much water have you got?	8. How many potatoes have you got?
9. How much sugar have you got?	10. How many eggs have you got?
11. How much cheese have you got?	12. How many burgers have you got?

Home and there is/are . . .

SESSION 23

Vocabulary and language structures

Lesson A: Rooms of the house (home)

a bathroom	a kitchen
a bedroom	a lounge
a hallway	a dining room
a garden	

Lesson B: Home vocabulary

bed	bedside table
toilet	sink
drawers	stairs

Lesson C: There is/there are

There is a sink in the bathroom.	There is an oven in the kitchen.
There are books in the bedroom.	There isn't a clock in the kitchen.
There isn't a fridge in the bathroom.	There aren't any windows in the hallway.

Lesson D: Is/are there. . . ? There are/aren't/is/isn't

Is there a sink in the bathroom? Yes, there is a sink in the bathroom.	Is there a bed in the bedroom? Yes, there is a bed in the bedroom.
Is there are toilet in the bedroom? No, there isn't a toilet in the bedroom.	Is/are there. . . ? (show a picture of a room with lots of things in it)
Are there any stairs in the hallway? Yes, there are some stairs in the hallway?	Are there any drawers in the bedroom? No, there aren't any drawers in the bedroom.

95

Also advised:

- Other home vocabulary.

Grammar rule: There isn't/aren't any

- We use 'There isn't/There aren't' to say somewhere, something doesn't exist, e.g. There isn't any sugar in the cupboard.
- We use 'any' when it doesn't matter which, e.g. any colour.
- We use 'There isn't any' when it doesn't matter which uncountable noun, e.g. There isn't any sugar.
- The short form for 'there is not' is 'there isn't.'
- We use 'There aren't any' when it doesn't matter which countable plural noun, e.g. There aren't any cars.
- The short form of 'There are not' is 'There aren't.'

Grammar rule: There is/are

- We use 'there is' to say somewhere, something exists, e.g. There is a car on the road.
- We use 'there is' for a singular noun, e.g. There is a car.
- We use 'there are' for a plural noun, e.g. There are cars.
- We often shorten 'there is' to 'there's.'

Lesson Resources A, vocabulary lesson: Rooms of the home

1. a bathroom	2. a kitchen
3. a bedroom	4. a lounge
5. a hallway	6. a dining room
7. a garden	

Lesson Resources B, vocabulary lesson: Home vocabulary

1. a bed	2. a bedside table
3. a toilet	4. a sink
5. some drawers	6. some stairs

© Caroline Scott (2020), *An English as an Additional Language (EAL) Programme: Learning Through Images for 7–14-Year-Olds*, Routledge

Lesson Resources C, language structure lesson: There is/there are

Cut out the following sentence ready for reconstruction.

There	is	a	sink	in
the	bathroom	.		

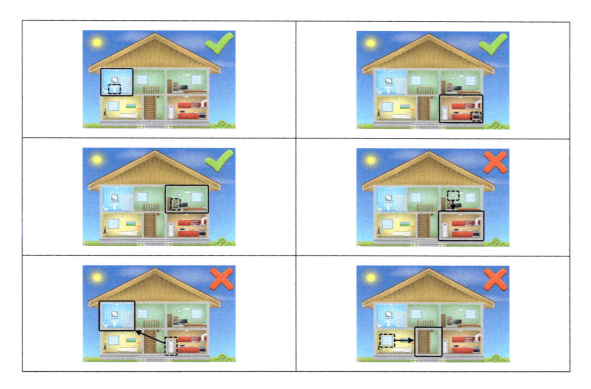

1. There is a sink in the bathroom.	2. There is an oven in the kitchen.
3. There are books in the bedroom.	4. There isn't a clock in the kitchen.
5. There isn't a fridge in the bathroom.	6. There aren't any windows in the hallway.

© Caroline Scott (2020), *An English as an Additional Language (EAL) Programme: Learning Through Images for 7–14-Year-Olds*, Routledge

SESSION 23

Lesson Resources D, language structure lesson: Is/are there. . . ? There are/aren't/is/isn't

Cut out the following sentence ready for reconstruction.

Is	there	a	sink	in
the	bathroom	?	Yes	,
there	is	a	sink	in
the	bathroom	.		

1. Is there a sink in the bathroom? Yes, there is a sink in the bathroom.	2. Is there a bed in the bedroom? Yes, there is a bed in the bedroom.
3. Is there a toilet in the bedroom? No, there isn't a toilet in the bedroom.	4. Are there any paintings in the bedroom? Yes, there are paintings in the bedroom.
5. Are there any stairs in the hallway? Yes, there are some stairs in the hallway?	6. Are there any drawers in the bedroom? No, there aren't any drawers in the bedroom.

100

© Caroline Scott (2020), *An English as an Additional Language (EAL) Programme: Learning Through Images for 7–14-Year-Olds*, Routledge

Prepositions

SESSION 24

Vocabulary and language structures

Lesson A: Prepositions

There is a pen above the box.	There is a pen next to the box.
There is a pen in front of the box.	There is a pen on the box.
There is a pen in the box.	There is a pen under the box.

Lesson B: There is/There are

There are some chairs under the table.	There are some pictures on the wall.
There is a rug on the floor.	There is a cupboard next to the toilet.

Also advised:

■ Talk about the classroom using prepositions of place.

Grammar rule: Prepositions of place

■ We use prepositions to describe position of something, e.g. The spider is under the cupboard.

101

Lesson Resources A, language structure lesson: Prepositions

Cut out the following sentence ready for reconstruction.

There	is	a	pen	above
the	box	.		

1. There is a pen above the box.	2. There is a pen next to the box.
3. There is a pen in front of the box.	4. There is a pen on the box.
5. There is a pen in the box.	6. There is a pen under the box.

© Caroline Scott (2020), *An English as an Additional Language (EAL) Programme: Learning Through Images for 7–14-Year-Olds*, Routledge

Lesson Resources B, language structure lesson: There is/There are

Cut out the following sentence ready for reconstruction.

There	are	some	chairs	under
the	table	.		

1. There are some chairs under the table.	2. There are some pictures on the wall.
3. There is a rug on the floor.	4. There is a cupboard next to the toilet.

SESSION 24

SESSION 25

Can/can't for permission

Vocabulary and language structures

Lesson A: Can for permission

Can I have a drink, please? Yes, you can.	Can I have a drink, please? No, you can't.
Can I watch TV, please? Yes, you can.	Can I watch TV, please? No, you can't.
Can I play on the computer, please? Yes, you can.	Can I play on the computer, please? No, you can't.
Can I buy that toy, please? Yes, you can.	Can I buy that toy, please? No, you can't.

Also use the language introduced in the pre-induction language section E, pages 25–26.

Also advised:

■ Can I have his/her . . . please?

Grammar rule: Can for permission

■ We use 'can' to ask for and give permission, e.g. Can I have a glass of orange juice, please?
■ We use 'cannot' (can't) to refuse permission, e.g. You can't have a glass of orange juice.

104

Lesson Resources A, language structure lesson: Can for permission

Cut out the following sentence ready for reconstruction.

Can	I	borrow	your	pen
,	please	?	Yes	,
you	can	.		

1. Can I have a drink, please? Yes, you can.	2. Can I have a drink, please? No, you can't.
3. Can I watch TV, please? Yes, you can.	4. Can I watch TV, please? No, you can't.

SESSION 25

SESSION 25

5. Can I play on the computer, please? No, you can't.	6. Can I play on the computer, please? Yes, you can.
7. Can I buy that toy, please? No, you can't.	8. Can I buy that toy, please? Yes, you can.

Do you/does he. . . ?

SESSION 26

Vocabulary and language structures

Lesson A: Do you/Does he

Do you eat meat? No, I don't.	Do you cook? Yes, I do?
Does he listen to music? Yes, she does.	Does she read? No, she doesn't.
Do they eat ice cream? Yes, they do.	Do we stand in a line? Yes, we do.

Also advised:

- Use 'do you. . .' examples for the learners' class, e.g. Do you sit at your table? Does she finish her homework?

Grammar rule: Do you like. . . ?

- We use 'do' to make questions with verbs, e.g. Do you like football?
- We use 'do' with 'I,' 'you,' 'they,' 'we,' e.g. Do you. . . ?
- We use 'does' with 'he,' 'she,' 'it,' a name, e.g. Does Caroline like football?

107

SESSION 26

Lesson Resources A, language structure lesson: Do you/Does he. . .

Cut out the following sentence ready for reconstruction.

| Do | you | eat | meat | ? |
| No | , | I | don't | . |

1. Do you eat meat? No, I don't.	2. Do you cook? Yes, I do?
3. Does he listen to music? Yes, he does.	4. Does she read? No, she doesn't.
5. Do they eat ice cream? Yes, they do.	6. Do we stand in a line? Yes, we do.

© Caroline Scott (2020), *An English as an Additional Language (EAL) Programme: Learning Through Images for 7–14-Year-Olds*, Routledge

Would you like . . . ?

SESSION 27

Vocabulary and language structures

Lesson A: I would like

What would you like? I would like some ham, please.	What would you like? I would like some cake, please.
What would you like? I would like a burger, please.	What would you like? I would like some pizza, please.
What would you like? I would like some orange juice, please.	What would you like? I would like some spaghetti, please.

Lesson B: Yes, I would

Would you like some water? Yes, I would, please.	Would you like some cake? No, I wouldn't, thank you.
Would you like some coffee? No, I wouldn't, thank you.	Would you like some cheese? No, I wouldn't, thank you.
Would you like some chips? No, I wouldn't, thank you.	Would you like some sausages? Yes, I would, please.

Also advised:

- Teach 'Sorry, I didn't hear you.' 'Can you say that again, please?'

Grammar rule: I would like. . .

- We can use 'would like' to offer something, invite someone or offer to do something, e.g. Would you like a drink?

109

SESSION 27

Lesson Resources A, language structure lesson: I would like...

Cut out the following sentence ready for reconstruction.

What	would	you	like	?
I	would	like	some	ham
,	please	.		

1. What would you like? I would like some ham, please.	2. What would you like? I would like some cake, please.
3. What would you like? I would like a burger, please.	4. What would you like? I would like some pizza, please.
5. What would you like? I would like some orange juice, please.	6. What would you like? I would like some spaghetti, please.

© Caroline Scott (2020), *An English as an Additional Language (EAL) Programme: Learning Through Images for 7–14-Year-Olds*, Routledge

Lesson Resources B, language structure lesson: Yes, I would.

Cut out the following sentence ready for reconstruction.

Would	you	like	some	water
?	Yes	,	I	would
,	please	.		

1. Would you like some water? Yes, I would, please.	2. Would you like some cake? No, I wouldn't, thank you.
3. Would you like some coffee? No, I wouldn't, thank you.	4. Would you like some cheese? No, I wouldn't, thank you.
5. Would you like some chips? No, I wouldn't, thank you.	6. Would you like some sausages? Yes, I would, please.

© Caroline Scott (2020), *An English as an Additional Language (EAL) Programme: Learning Through Images for 7–14-Year-Olds*, Routledge

Feelings

SESSION 28

Vocabulary and language structures

Lesson A: Feelings

I'm cold.	I'm bored.
I'm tired.	I'm late.
I'm thirsty.	I'm hungry.

Lesson B: Wants and feelings

She is cold. She wants to be warm.	He is thirsty. He wants some water.
He is tired. He wants to go to sleep.	He is wet. He wants to be dry.
She is hungry. She wants to eat.	He is bored. He wants to play.

Also advised:

- Consider other wants and what the feelings might be.

Grammar rule: I want. . .

- We use 'want' to say what we feel a need, wish or desire for, e.g. I want a drink.
- Want can be followed by object + infinitive, e.g. You want me to go.

Lesson Resources A, vocabulary lesson: Feelings

SESSION 28

1. I'm cold.	2. I'm hot
3. I'm tired	4. I'm late.
5. I'm thirsty.	6. I'm hungry.

Lesson Resources B, language structure lesson: Wants and feelings

Cut out the following sentence ready for reconstruction.

She	is	cold	.	She
wants	to	be		
warm	.			

1. She is cold. She wants to be warm.	2. He is thirsty. He wants some water.
3. He is tired. He wants to go to sleep.	4. He is wet. He wants to be dry.
5. She is hungry. She wants to eat.	6. He is bored. He wants to play.

© Caroline Scott (2020), *An English as an Additional Language (EAL) Programme: Learning Through Images for 7–14-Year-Olds*, Routledge

Shops and places

SESSION 29

Vocabulary and language structures

Lesson A: Places

school	shop
cafe	newsagents
house	bank

Lesson A: Where is/are. . . ?

Where is the waterfall? It is behind the bridge.	Where is the yellow house? It is next to the red houses.
Where is the shop? It is under the house.	Where is the office? It is on the corner of the street.
Where is the door? It is in front of the house.	Where is your house? It is next to the red house.

Also advised:

- Teach prepositions around the school, e.g. What is next to your classroom? What is opposite the toilet?

Grammar rule: Where is/are. . . ?

- We use 'where' to ask about a place.
- We use 'where is' to ask about one place, e.g. Where is the swimming pool?
- We use 'where are' to ask about more than one place, e.g. Where are the shops?

Grammar rule: Prepositions of place

- We use prepositions to describe position, e.g. It is next to the red house.

115

Lesson Resources A, vocabulary lesson: Places

1. school	2. shop
3. café	4. newsagents
5. house	6. bank

Lesson Resources A, language structure lesson: Where is/are. . . ?

Cut out the following sentence ready for reconstruction.

Where	is	the	waterfall	?
It	is	behind	the	bridge
.				

1. Where is the waterfall? It is behind the bridge.	2. Where is the yellow house? It is between the red houses.
3. Where is the shop? It is under the house.	4. Where is the office? It is on the corner of the street.
5. Where is the door? It is at the front of the house.	6. Where is your house? It is next to the red house.

© Caroline Scott (2020), *An English as an Additional Language (EAL) Programme: Learning Through Images for 7–14-Year-Olds*, Routledge

Directions

SESSION 30

Vocabulary and language structures

Lesson A: Directions

Turn left	Turn right
Go straight on	Second on right
On the corner	First on left

Lesson B: Where is . . .

Where is the museum? Go straight on and take the second road on your left. It is then on your right.	Where is the hospital? Turn right and go straight on and it's opposite you.
Where is your flat? Go straight on and it's the second block of flats on your right.	Where is the church? Go straight on. Take the second road on your right and then again take the second road on your right. It's on your left.
Where is the library? Take a right and then a left. Go straight on and take the second road on your right. It is then on your left.	

Also advised:

- Teach directions around the school, e.g. How do you get to the toilet?

Lesson Resources A, vocabulary lesson: Directions

1. turn left	2. turn right
3. go straight on	4. second on right
5. on the corner	6. first on left

© Caroline Scott (2020), *An English as an Additional Language (EAL) Programme: Learning Through Images for 7–14-Year-Olds*, Routledge

SESSION 30

Lesson Resources B, vocabulary lesson: Where is. . .

1. Where is the museum? Go straight on and take the second road on your left. It is then on your right.	2. Where is the hospital? Turn right and go straight on and it's opposite you.
3. Where is your flat? Go straight on and it's the second block of flats on your right.	4. Where is the church? Go straight on. Take the second road on your right and then again take the second road on your right. It's on your left.
5. Where is the library? Take a right and then a left. Go straight on and take the second road on your right. It is then on your left.	

120

© Caroline Scott (2020), *An English as an Additional Language (EAL) Programme: Learning Through Images for 7–14-Year-Olds*, Routledge

Next steps for beginner learners. . .

The following sessions show the continuing learning journey. You can source your own images for these or access them and additional curriculum related language in the Learning Village (www.learningvillage.net).

Session	Lesson name	Example	Language Learning challenge
31. Clothes	Clothes	a belt	Clothes vocabulary (Articles 'a/an')
	Adjectives	patterned	Adjectives to describe material
	Describing clothes	a long belt	Adjectives to describe material (Clothes vocabulary)
	How many	How many pairs of stripy socks do you have? I have three pairs of stripy socks.	Language structure 'How many. . .?' 'I have . . .' (Language structure 'Which one?')
32. Money	Money	£1 = one pound	Money – GBP
	Shopping	a bar code	Shopping vocabulary
	How much is/are	How much are the biscuits?	Verb to be 'are/is' (Language structure 'How much')
	They are/It is	How much are the biscuits? They are £1.50.	Language structure 'They are/It is' (Language structure 'How much')
	I'll buy. . .	I'll buy the pants. The blue ones.	Vocabulary 'ones' (Language structure 'I'll buy')
33. Time 1	Time vocabulary	little hand	Time vocabulary
	O'clock	What's the time? It's 5 o'clock.	Language structure 'It's __ o'clock.' (Language structure 'What's the time?')
	Half past	What's the time? It's half past 5.	Language structure 'It's half past . . .' (Language structure 'What's the time?')
	Quarter past	What's the time? It's quarter past 5.	Language structure 'It's quarter past . . .' (Language structure 'What's the time?')
	Quarter to	What's the time? It's quarter to 2.	Language structure 'It's quarter to . . .' (Language structure 'What's the time?')
	Quarter past, quarter to, o'clock and half past	What's the time? It's 3 o'clock.	Language structure 'quarter past/quarter to/o'clock/half past' (What's the time?)
34. Daily routine	Daily routine	He brushes his teeth.	Daily routine vocabulary
	Time of the day and year – in a time	in the afternoon	Time 'in' (Time indicators)

SESSION 30

Session	Lesson name	Example	Language Learning challenge
	Time of the day and year – at a time	at night	Time 'at' (Time indicators)
	Prepositions – at or in	He reads at 2 o'clock.	Time 'at/in' (Time indicators)
35. Days of the week	Days of the week	on Thursday	Days of the week vocabulary (Preposition 'on')
36. Adverbs of frequency	Adverbs of frequency	He never plays sport.	Adverbs of frequency (Sports vocabulary)
	Adverbs of frequency, daily routine and in, on, at	He usually reads in the afternoons.	Adverbs of frequency (Prepositions 'on/in/at')
37. Time 2	Time 5 past	5 past 2	Time '5 past'
	Time 10 past	10 past 2	Time '10 past'
	Time 20 past	20 past 3	Time '20 past'
	Time 25 past	25 past 4	Time '25 past'
	Time 5 to	5 to 1	Time '5 to'
	Time 10 to	10 to 2	Time '10 to'
	Time 20 to	20 to 10	Time '20 to'
	Time 25 to	25 to 1	Time '25 to'
38. How often do you	Time markers	once	Time markers
	How often do you . . .?	How often do you take the bus? I take the bus once a week.	Time markers (Language structure 'How often do you . . .?')
39. Time revision	Daily routine and time	He brushes his teeth at 5 to 7.	Time (Daily routine vocabulary)
	Adverbs of frequency, daily routine and time	When do they usually have dinner with the family? They usually have dinner with the family at 25 to 8.	Time (Language structure 'When does he usually . . .?')
40. Body 1	Body	an ankle	Body parts vocabulary
41. Feelings	How are you feeling?	How are you feeling? I am feeling angry.	Feelings vocabulary (Language structure 'How are you feeling?')
	Do you feel	Do you feel happy? No, I don't.	'No, I don't./Yes, I do.' (Language structure 'Do you feel . . .?')

122

Session	Lesson name	Example	Language Learning challenge
42. Illness	Illness	a cold	Illnesses vocabulary
	I have	I have a cold.	Illnesses vocabulary
	Hurts	My elbow hurts.	Illnesses vocabulary (Language structure 'I have a/an . . .')
43. Cures	Cures	put a plaster on it	Cures vocabulary
	What's the matter?	What's the matter? My knee hurts. Put a plaster on it.	Cures vocabulary (Language structure 'What's the matter?')
44. Transport	Transport	a bicycle	Transport vocabulary
	I go by	I go by bicycle.	Preposition 'by' (Transport vocabulary)
45. Jobs	Jobs	a doctor	Jobs vocabulary
	I am a	I am a singer.	Jobs vocabulary (Language structure 'I am a/an')
46. How do you get to	He is a	What does he do? He is a farmer.	Language structure 'He is/ are . . .' (Language structure 'What does he do?')
	How do you get to work?	How does he get to work? He gets to work by tractor.	Third person singular 'get/gets' (Preposition 'by')
47. What is he doing?	present continuous +ing	We are talking.	Present continuous ('is/am/are')
	What is he doing?	What is he doing? He is kicking the ball.	Present continuous ('What is she doing?')
48. Why are you going?	Because	He is not cleaning the dishes because he is late.	Conjunction 'because'
	Why	Why are you late? My train was delayed.	Interrogative adverb 'why' (Past tense verb be 'was/were')
49. Shape	Shape names	a circle	Shape vocabulary
	Adjectives to describe patterns	Checked	Adjectives to describe patterns
	What shape is it?	What shape is it? It's square shaped.	How objects are shaped (Interrogative pronoun 'what')
	What colour is it?	It's striped.	Adjectives to describe patterns (Contraction 'it's')

SESSION 30

Session	Lesson name	Example	Language Learning challenge
50. Past tense – was/were	Time indicators	last year	Time indicators
	Was, were	On Tuesday he was eating a hamburger.	Past tense verb to be 'was/were' (Time indicators)
51. Past tense – there was/were	Home 2	a burglar	Home vocabulary
	There, was, were	There was a burglar.	Past tense language structure with to be 'There was/were' (Home vocabulary)
52. Past tense – ed	Verbs 1	to like	Basic verbs
	Past tense verbs 1 – regular verbs	In 2012 she tied her wedding dress.	Past tense verbs '-ed'
	Verbs 2	to argue	Basic verbs
	Past tense verbs 2 – regular verbs	At 2 o'clock we talked.	Past tense verbs '-ed'
	Verbs 3	to ask	Basic verbs
	Past tense verbs 3 – regular verbs	He asked the teacher on Monday.	Past tense verbs '-ed'
53. Past tense – ir-regular	Verbs 4	to light	Basic verbs
	Past tense verbs 4 – irregular verbs	I lit a match yesterday evening.	Past tense irregular verbs
	Verbs 5	to teach	Basic verbs
	Past tense verbs 5 – irregular verbs	He taught yesterday.	Past tense irregular verbs
54. Past tense – did	Past tense – did not	He did not close the door.	Past tense 'did not'
	Past tense verbs – did and didn't	He didn't play football yesterday.	Past tense 'did/didn't' (Time markers)
55. Past tense – did 2	Did you . . .? 2	Did he close the door? No, he didn't.	Past tense 'Did you . . .?' 'Yes, I did/No, I didn't.'
	Did you . . .?	Did you play football yesterday? Yes, I did.	Past tense 'Did you . . .?' 'Yes, I did/No, I didn't.'
56. Months	Months	January	Months vocabulary
	Months 2	January is month 1	Numbers of the months (Months vocabulary)

Session	Lesson name	Example	Language Learning challenge
57. Past tense – had	Had – have 1	Last week she had an ice cream.	Past tense 'have/had' (Time markers)
	Had – have 2	Last week she had an ice cream. This week she has a hamburger.	Past tense 'have/had' (Time markers)
58. Adverbs	Verbs	to cut	Basic verbs
	Adverbs	to cut dangerously	Adverbs
59. Must	Must	You must walk on the path.	Model verb 'must'
	Must not	You must not use your phone.	Model verb 'must not'
	Must – must not	You must cross on a zebra crossing.	Model verb 'must, mustn't'
60. Because . . . so	Because	He bought her a present because they had a fight.	Conjunction 'because' (Past tense verbs)
	Because, so	He bought her a present because they had a fight, so they made friends again.	Conjunctions 'because,' 'so' (Past tense verbs)
61. Have to	Have to	You have to recycle your rubbish.	Language structure 'have to' (Imperatives)
	Have to – don't have to	You don't have to wake up early.	Language structure 'don't have to/have to' (imperatives)
62. Weather	Weather	It's cloudy.	Weather vocabulary (Contraction 'It's')
	What's the weather like?	What's the weather like? It's cloudy.	Weather vocabulary (Language structure 'What's the weather like?')
63. Weather – going to	Time markers – future	next month	Future time markers
	Going to	The day after tomorrow, it's going to be cloudy with sunny spells.	Going to (Future time markers)
	Countries 1	America	Countries vocabulary
	Countries 2	India	Countries vocabulary
	What's the weather going to be like?	What's the weather going to be like? In China it's going to be hot.	Language structure 'going to' (Countries vocabulary)

Session	Lesson name	Example	Language Learning challenge
64. What's going to happen?	What's going to happen? 1	He is going to get wet.	Language structure 'going to'
	What's going to happen? 2	He is going to fall asleep.	Language structure 'going to'
65. What will happen?	Will	My mum will go shopping next week.	Modal verb 'will' (Future time markers)
66. Perhaps	Perhaps	Perhaps I will go travelling.	Adverb 'perhaps' (Modal verb 'will/'ll/won't')
	Will/Going to	He is going to help her.	Modal verb 'will/going to'
67. Comparatives and superlatives	Comparatives, superlatives	big ball, bigger ball, biggest ball	Comparatives/superlatives '-er/-est'
68. Comparatives and superlatives	Comparatives, superlatives	beautiful lady, more beautiful lady, most beautiful lady	Comparatives/superlatives 'more/most'
	Comparatives, superlatives	good runner	Irregular comparatives/superlatives

These sessions also align to 'Teaching English as an Additional Language 5-11: A Whole School Resource' by Caroline Scott and the Learning Village (www.learningvillage.net) which both provide additional supportive resources.

4
EAL framework

Considering the requirements of EAL learners at a variety of stages of English language acquisition and mother tongue development is a challenge. School-wide adaptations are necessary.

The opinion that learners with limited English proficiency should easily slip into the English-speaking mainstream with teachers providing limited adjustment for language learning requirements is controversial.

> Some assume that the more exposure to English the students have, the more quickly they will reach the desired English language proficiency level. The reality is that this assumption is not true. Most LEP/ELL [Limited English proficient/English Language Learners] need a specialized instructional mode to enable them to learn English while at the same time advancing in other curriculum areas.
>
> (Carrasquillo and Rodriguez, 2002)

Not only do learners with limited English proficiency not have the communicative and academic English language skills to access the curriculum, but teachers and school leaders are often also used to working with a curriculum that doesn't explicitly address EAL learners' needs. They therefore feel particularly under-skilled. Additionally, in some circumstances learners can immediately feel excluded. They are often unable to access the learning and therefore, unable to be successful and low self-esteem can develop.

> Students feel they are not part of the instructional setting and their self-image may be negatively affected. Since a person's self-esteem is constantly re-evaluated on the basis of new encounters and experiences, as LEP students enter the school they will engage in many new social interactions that will enhance or lower their self-esteem.
>
> (Carrasquillo and Rodriguez, 2002)

Therefore, what kind of adjustments should be made? Where do you start?

This summary of the Across Cultures EAL framework is designed to provide some starting points for developing a whole-school approach to adjusting to learners in transition and beyond.

EAL Framework for whole school development

Developing a whole school commitment to EAL requires a collaborative effort. Working parties nominated to focus on particular areas can promote a shared vision, increase urgency, empower a range of staff, build focused teamwork and focus staff on constructive short and long-term goals.

This framework provides a structured starting point to support EAL development across the school.

Framework strands	Self-assessment questions
Strand 1: Understanding EAL learners in the mainstream	1a. Have all staff **experienced what it feels like** to learn a foreign language without translation? 1b. Do teachers know **major factors hindering English language proficiency**? 1c. Do teachers **know why and how to support learners' mother tongue**?
Strand 2: Enhanced admissions, including community building	2a. Do **enhanced admission procedures** include questions on proficiency in other languages, development of their mother tongue, reasons for transition, periods without schools, life prior to arrival and cultural expectations of school life? 2b. Is there a **procedure for communicating appropriate** admissions information to teachers and other staff? 2c. Is a **welcome procedure** in place, e.g. teaching the learner how to ask for things, pointing out where things are, telling the learner what they will be learning, noting how the learner and parents can assist (and how the teachers can continue to communicate with parents, etc.)? 2d Are **buddies trained**, e.g. in how to offer support and how and when to translate? 2e. Are **parents included** in family learning or are there parent transition activities on arrival to support their own transition?
Strand 3: EAL assessment	3a. Is **evidence used to assess EAL learners** using an EAL assessment continuum which identifies next steps in learning from absolute beginner through to fluent? 3b. Are **new-to-English learners assessed** on arrival and termly for: – Reading (and phonics where appropriate) – Writing – Speaking and listening – Vocabulary and language structures 3c. Are EAL learners **actively involved in assessing their language learning**? 3d. Are EAL learners **given appropriate feedback** on their learning? 3e. Are **ongoing informal assessments** and the **EAL continuum used** to inform learning?
Strand 4: Induction-to-English	4a. Do new-to-English learners have consistent access to appropriate, progressive, well-resourced, collaborative **everyday language learning** lessons, alongside mainstream lessons? 4b. Do learners **access collaborative activities** that build confidence and a sense of belonging? 4c. Do class teachers and parents **know what learning is taking place** during new-to-English induction? 4d. Is **assessment for learning integral** to the induction lessons? 4e. Do learners have **access to short, well-paced phonics** sessions? 4f. Where possible, do induction lessons align or **link to the school curriculum**? 4g. Do learners have some **clear strategies to support their language learning** beyond the classroom?
Differentiating for EAL learners in class Note: The questions in strands 5 & 6 apply to a series of lessons.	
Strand 5: Planning differentiation for EAL learners in class	5a. Are **content-learning challenges** identified? 5b. Are **language-learning challenges** identified? 5c. Is the **content suitable for age and language background**? 5d. Does it include **appropriate, comprehensible learning opportunities** for learning curriculum concepts? 5e. Are there planned opportunities to access **higher-order thinking skills**? 5f. Is the **progression of learning suitably presented**?

Framework strands	Self-assessment questions
	5g. If reading is present, are **reading activities appropriately levelled** so they are comprehensible, yet appropriate for reaching the content learning challenge? 5e. Are **resources suitably selected** to be adaptable to the language and content needs of EAL learners at every level of proficiency? (E.g. use of graphic organizers, visuals and so on) 5f. Are learners **grouped appropriately** for learning?
Strand 6: Differentiating for EAL learners in class Key focuses	Integral elements 6a. Does the session provide **appropriate comprehensible** input to all learners from any language background? For example, is there clear modelling with a variety of demonstration from practical work, visuals, gestures, or collaborative learning? 6b. Does the session include opportunities to **access higher-order thinking skills**? For example, does the teaching introduce appropriate curriculum concepts or enable questioning? 6c. Are **opportunities for speaking and listening integral** to the session? 6d. Is time allowed for clarification of learning and a **variety of feedback**? (E.g. peer feedback, teacher feedback, self-assessment?) 6e. Is the session **paced appropriately** for all ability levels? Connection (orientate, assess & build the field) 6f. Does the session **build on learners' prior knowledge**? 6g. If appropriate, is **revision of previous concepts**, vocabulary or language structures built into the connection activity? 6h. Is **questioning used to initiate thinking**, engage and hypothesize about the concept? (This may include pre-taught vocabulary and language structures.) Activation (explore, model & jointly construct) 6i. Do all learners **explore the content learning challenge**? 6j. Does the activity provide **clear, structured, modelling/scaffolding** & **result in joint construction**? 6k. Are **vocabulary and language structures highlighted** clearly so that learners of all language abilities can access the content? 6l. Are **language learning strategies modelled** to support learners in accessing content? (E.g. using a substitution table for speaking or writing, or a strategy for remembering vocabulary or highlighting words they don't know to add to a homework activity.) Demonstration (refine, practice & move to independence) 6m. Are learners of all language abilities **using the vocabulary and language structures** highlighted to access the content? 6n. Are learners using the **clear structure or scaffold provided** to access the learning? 6o. Are EAL learners using the **language learning strategies modelled** to support them in accessing content? 6p. If writing is present, are **opportunities provided to rehearse the language** before writing occurs? Consolidation (revise, apply & reflect) 6q. Can the learner apply the learning to **real-life experiences**?

Framework strands	Self-assessment questions
	6r. Is there a **review of all vocabulary and language structures** learnt? 6s. Are all learners able to **reflect on their content learning**? (Prior modelling of appropriate vocabulary and language structures can support learners of all abilities in articulating themselves.)
Strand 7: Focused scaffolding of language to support comprehensible input	7a. Are **everyday, technical and academic vocabulary and language structures** (language form – the grammatical structure of words and phrases as well as the word themselves) **scaffolded** to support comprehensible input? 7b. Is the **language function** (what learners do with language as they engage with it, e.g. evaluate) scaffolded to support comprehensible input? 7c. Are learners **using new vocabulary in a variety of ways** and moving it into their receptive repertoire? 7d. Are learners **pre-learning vocabulary and language structures?** 7e. Are **suitable teaching methods and strategies** used to support learning vocabulary and language structures? E.g. writing frames or substitution tables. 7f. Is there **appropriate grouping for supporting focused scaffolding**?
Strand 8: Supportive use of language learning strategies, including extended reading, writing, speaking & listening	8a. Is there provision for ongoing **accessible guided and free voluntary reading**? 8b. Are there continued opportunities for curriculum-related **extended, creative writing** based on initial scaffolding? 8c. Are there ongoing opportunities for role play, drama and other **collaborative speaking and listening activities**? 8d. Is there **ongoing use of language learning strategies** that are effective at **supporting learners in taking ownership of their language learning** and **teachers and parents in supporting language learning?** 8e. Are there **ongoing use of language learning strategies** that are effective at **supporting groups of learners** in furthering their language development?
Strand 9: Whole school EAL development	9a. Does the working party **empower a range of staff,** including school leaders, working as a team? 9b. Is there a **shared vision for EAL**? 9c. Are there **manageable short- and long-term goals** set for developing provision for EAL? 9d. Will the EAL working party **develop formal guidelines,** e.g. an EAL development plan, EAL handbook and updated policy?

Source: Across Cultures EAL Framework for Whole School Development, Caroline Scott, 2019

For more supporting resources, templates and training on the Across Cultures EAL Framework, see: www.axcultures.com/framework. Based on 'Teaching English as an Additional Language: A Whole School Resource' Caroline Scott, 2012

Guidance on differentiation for EAL learners in class

Figure 4.1 is strand 7 from the EAL framework (presented earlier) showing the learning cycle in a session (a series of lessons). It provides an example of the main considerations needed to accommodate for EAL learners in the mainstream (most, if not all, are beneficial to all learners).

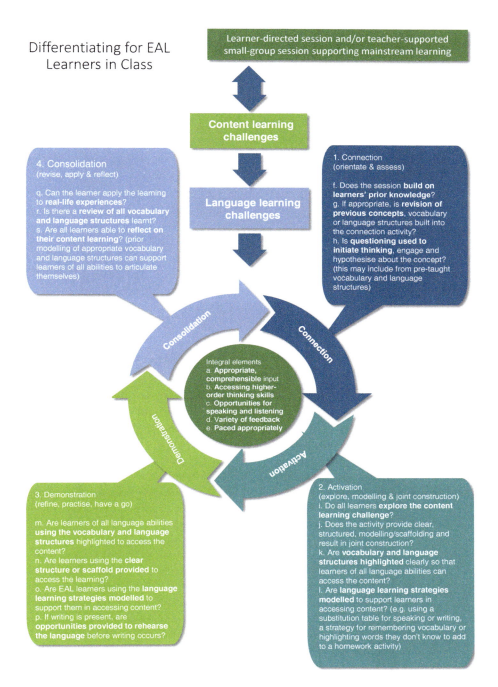

Figure 4.1 Differentiating for EAL learners in class, EAL Framework: Strand 7
Source: www.axcultures.com/framework

Class teaching with international new arrivals is most definitely a challenge. Learners are often learning to be literate in their own language at the same time as beginning their transition to using English as a medium of instruction. Alongside this, they need to be accessing cognitively engaging content in English despite their limited grasp of the language as well as maintaining their mother tongue.

> For English language learners, this high challenge classroom must be one where they are given the kinds of scaffolding and linguistic support that will enable them to engage in learning and be successful learners, in terms of both their English language development and the development of subject knowledge.
>
> (Gibbons, 2009)

Suggestions

Use of mother tongue

Learners need to be encouraged to use their mother tongue to support learning. "It ensures that students' cognitive development continues alongside the learning of the new language" (Sears, 2015). Ask learners to make notes in their mother tongue in their books to support their understanding (see p. 48 for more strategies).

Assessing prior knowledge

Learning challenges need to be accessible and based on prior knowledge and experience. "When the brain encounters a new idea, it searches for prior knowledge and similar experiences" (Lombardi, 2008). To provide learning that is accessible and based on prior knowledge, a thorough assessment of learners' starting points needs to guide teaching and learning choices. Although initial assessment is necessary and helpful, ongoing assessment for learning will offers the real-time feedback from learners that will most likely underpin ongoing teaching and learning choices.

Share the rationale

> The search for meaning is innate . . . . When teachers share with students a rationale for what they are doing, the brain and learner more deeply value the learning.
>
> (Lombardi, 2008)

The teacher thus needs to be specific about the goals for a lesson. Learners may explore a topic to develop interest, however, they need to present the language-learning so learners have the tools to communicate their understanding. It can be useful to put the language-learning objective on the board at the start of every lesson and consistently make it the title or subtitle of the learners' work.

Pre-teaching

Much can be identified and covered in various ways prior to the lesson. Lombardi (2008) highlights the use of "front-loading – pre-teaching, modeling, and rehearsing key concepts, skills and terms" for English language learners. This 'front-loading' can be provided in small-group support, as homework or in carefully selected independent learning time during the school day.

> Schools that established high levels of pupil self-esteem by celebrating even the smallest of gains or by the practice of 'pre-teaching' a concept or skill to a group or individual prior to whole class teaching, were able to demonstrate positive outcomes for pupils. As were those which concentrated on improving pupils' attitudes to learning.
>
> (Wilson, J. and Carmel Education Trust, 2014)

Teachers should ask themselves:

- What can I do to support the learners before the session begins? (pre-learning content [maybe in their home language [and learning key words and phrases in English)
- Can the learner's family help in their home language with content learning as a part of pre-teaching?
- What vocabulary and language structures can this learner successfully use to access the content?

Use of substitution tables

Try using a substitution table to help with spoken then written language. For example, the learning challenge may be to know about the holiday destination. The activity may be to launch a new television advert to attract visitors to travel to that destination. The language learning focus may be on creating a sentence using persuasive adjectives and the use of articles 'a/an.'

		article	*adjective*	
A holiday like this	*will offer you*	a/an	exciting	adventure
			wonderful	
			incredible	

Higher ability learners could focus on other elements of the language, like the connectives or other ways to describe the holiday using nouns.

				noun	*connective*
A holiday like this	*will offer you*	a/an	exiting	adventure	because...
	provides you with		wonderful	challenge	therefore...
	gives		incredible	experience	
				opportunity	

Scaffolding

Scaffolding, in this case, is a process a teacher uses to model and jointly reconstruct language in order to help learners articulate themselves independently. After modelling, they step back, offering support as needed.

The teacher should ask themselves:

- Have I scaffolded the genres the learner is accessing?
- Did this start with speaking and listening activities and accessing new vocabulary and suitable language structures as well as purpose, organisation and features before any writing began?

Gibbons (2009) presents a teaching and learning cycle to scaffold writing:

Stage 1: Building the field

This is primarily content focused which aims to build-up information about the topic itself. The use of the home language to research this area can be very helpful. There's a lot that can be done before the topic as research in their own language.

Stage 2: Modelling Genre

This stage is focused on the form and function of the language in the genre. Learner can become familiar with the purpose, organization and language features of the genre.

Stage 3: Joint construction

This stage is focused on both content and language. Students and teacher can write together 'shared writing' to create a model. Whilst doing this, teacher and students can point out why they chose (or didn't choose) words, functions and features to support their future independent decision making.

Stage 4: Independent writing

Learners then have a go themselves in a first draft. It's vital learners refer to the joint construction and there is feedback maybe from a peer or a teacher. They should be encouraged or reread their writing and check for errors. Note that the earlier language learners may require more scaffolding.

Modes of collaboration

Differentiating curriculum content should expose learners to accessible, varied context driven language use. Although a single teacher can provide significant support, learning does not need to be solely their responsibility. Collaborative teaching methods to support the learner with their language learning can be a very efficient way to address this. Creese (2005) outlines some modes of collaboration, see Figures 4.2a and 4.2b:

- Observational and advisory support
- Subject teacher-directed curriculum for whole class teachers: targeting different students
- EAL teacher directed curriculum for bilingual students: teachers targeting different students

133

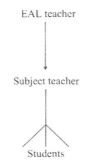

3.1. Observational and advisory support

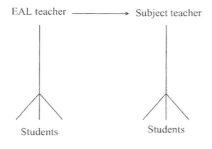

3.2. Subject teacher-directed curriculum for whole class: teachers targeting different students

3.3. EAL teacher directed curriculum for bilingual students: teachers targeting different students

3.4. In-class language support with no consultation between teachers

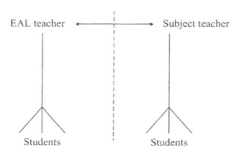

3.5. Temporary withdrawal with teachers informing one another of materials covered

Figure 4.2 'Ten modes of collaboration', from 'Teacher Collaboration and Talk in Multilingual Classrooms' by Angela Creese

Source: A. Creese 2005

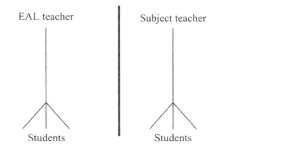

3.6. Permanent withdrawal – teachers not in discussion about materials and curriculum covered. Students disapplied from subject examination

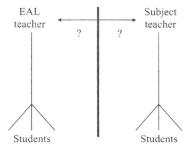

3.7. ESL Option Class

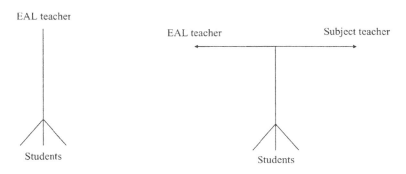

3.8. Language induction programme

3.9. Partnership teaching

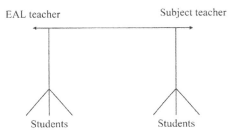

3.10. Partnership teaching with teachers targeting different students

Figure 4.2 Continued

- In-class language support with no consultation between teachers
- Temporary withdrawal with teachers informing one another of materials covered
- Permanent withdrawal – teachers not in discussion about materials and curriculum covered. Students disapplied from subject examinations.
- ESL option class
- Language induction programme
- Partnership teaching
- Partnership teaching with teachers targeting different students

Creese (2005)

Some of these methods may not be appropriate for suitable learner integration into the mainstream, e.g. 4.2b

3.6 Permanent withdrawal, so careful thought should be applied to achieve the best possible model with the staffing available.

Conclusion

Whatever the whole school approach to including EAL learners, school leaders need to actively support teachers in developing the skills they need to teach language alongside content in all lessons. The task of differentiating for EAL in the mainstream is challenging and time-consuming, but with practice, and the right support, delivering this kind of provision gives learners the tools they need to engage in curriculum concepts and enables them to make the progress they richly deserve alongside their more fluent peers.

5
Including families

Parents arriving at a school with international new arrivals are often undergoing a similar transition to their child. In a possibly unknown culture operating in an unknown language and sometimes with little or no members of a community who speak the same language around them, parents need support too. These families have a significantly larger transition to make. The challenge of including these parents, as with their children, can be hindered by language barriers and notably, a cultural background which may have very different expectations on how a school works with parents.

The first or second meeting the parent has with the school is the teacher's opportunity to source a translator (if the parent is not able to come with a friend or community member who can translate). They can then form good mutual expectations of learning developed from clear starting points. Without this initial meeting, some parents lack connection with the school, and learners' potential needs can go unnoticed for months due to assumptions that issues may be due to their limited English. This is a good time to ask a few questions about their child's language development in their mother tongue to highlight possible issues that might later be clouded by the language barrier.

Example questions to ask about their child:

- What language do they speak to different family members?
- Are they literate in their mother tongue?
- Did they develop their mother tongue at a similar rate to their peers?
- What are their interests?
- What age was your child when first introduced to English?

It's your chance to explain:

- the immense challenges their child will face during their transition
- what their child will be learning
- what their child can expect during the school day

- a clear system for how to support their child
- the importance of valuing and maintaining their mother tongue
- the importance of stability at home
- the importance of supporting friendships
- how the parent can become part of the school community

It is advisable to meet regularly with a parent in the initial weeks. A quick meeting with the learner and family member can be held at the end of the school day where there is an exchange of comments on the learning (maybe through a learner's Remember Book, see Chapter 2). This will foster home learning, a good rapport and offer a chance for you or the parent to raise any concerns or highlight achievements. It also shows the learner that you and their parents are working together.

Family learning

Families in transition need to be included, and welcoming parents into their new community with collaborative learning (family learning) can have a powerful effect on parental support and involvement in school and wider life in future months.

Parental or family involvement will help you to understand more about the learner's life as well as build a valuable rapport and level of trust between all involved. It also provides the parents with greater reason to learn English, an opportunity to ask questions, a chance to give them ownership of strategies for supporting their children at home, the opportunity to understand the school standards or expectations and even a chance to help the parent understand how a system in school or beyond might work in this new country.

Helen Adams, a Headteacher and former EAL advisor, gave some pertinent examples, "I have known families from countries where failing students repeat the year, who assume their child is doing really well because they are moving up each year. I have also had discussions with parents in European countries where children start formal

137

education later, who didn't realise that an 8-year-old reading at book band level 5 was 3 years behind this age related expectation in England. Similarly, mothers who have only had a rudimentary primary education and thinking that a few sentences in Y6 was good."

The National Learning and Work Institute (2018) completed a randomized controlled trial of a Community-Based English Language intervention aimed at people with very low levels of functional English proficiency. Findings showed "a strong and clear positive impact that attendance on an intensive 11-week Community-Based English Language course has on both English proficiency and social integration for those with relatively low levels of English proficiency" (Integrated Communities English Language Programme, 2018). We shouldn't underestimate the power of building a community.

One school in Peterborough, UK, was dominated by 50% EAL learners with a high number of new Roma families with a significant difference in social or educational experience to the UK. The school identified that these families mistrusted the school and did not see the significance of education. They also tended to have low self-esteem and self-perception.

The school aimed to raise the awareness and profile of this group, raise their aspirations and fill gaps in understanding the system. They managed to engage many of these parents through the efforts they made to link with the community. This included recruiting a Roma Governor from the community and working with local role models from the Roma community. The school took the Roma learners on trips to show them what they could achieve. They also worked towards raising the profile of this group amongst the staff. Mentoring for individual students and families was also a significant part of their programme. In addition, they tailored the curriculum to suit the learning needs of these groups by focusing on developing academic, linguistic and social development (Driver, 2018).

For more information on Roma families contact, Compass, www.compas.org.uk

Family learning framework

This family learning framework is designed to:

- Build rapport between the parent and the school (breaking down language and cultural barriers)
- Build capacity for the parent to support their child
- Welcome parents into the community
- Encourage parental engagement in the school community

The framework consists of a series of lessons to be delivered by a teacher in the school to the parents with little or no English. Internal teachers provide significant inside understanding of the school (events, curriculum, children, school agreements and procedures, school trips) as well as usual connections with staff, which has substantial value over employing external ESOL (English to speakers of Other Languages) teachers.

The sessions include learning with their child. It is beneficial to involve the child in learning with their parent to encourage them to work together, give the parents ideas on how to support their child at home, give you an insight into how to best support them and to show the learner that the school is working in partnership with parents. It also promotes attendance as parents and younger children (especially those under 11) are often keen to work together in the school setting.

These sessions are focused on the language parents need to navigate the school system. Joanna Clarke, an ESOL teacher delivering family learning, mentioned some of the key areas she focusses on:

- parts of the school, e.g. names of field, dinner hall, etc.
- homework tips
- tips on how to read with your child
- tips on the importance of retaining home language
- information on school holidays and important dates during the year
- library information and bilingual book availability
- information on clubs
- information on secondary transfer system and how secondary schools are different
- conversations with the office staff, e.g. regarding dinner money, trip money, sickness
- conversations with the teacher, e.g. about parents' evenings, trip details, medical needs, friendship issues, concerns over, e.g. where learner sits, etc.
- rewards and sanctions
- items on the school news letter
- information on assessment, e.g. SATs testing

    Joanna Clarke, ESOL teacher, Hillbrook Primary

English for parents in schools (absolute beginners)

Family Learning framework

You can teach beginners of English and/or Family Learning (for parents who are more fluent) through this framework. It is designed to create a rapport between the school and parents, develop a supportive community, build friendships, offer insight into how the school works and how they can get involved and provide some supportive school-related English classes. Parts A and B can be used weekly (A followed by B) or in isolation (e.g. A or B only). For more resources to go with this programme, see: www. communityvillage.net.

	A. Framework for teaching English to parents in schools (beginners)		*B. Family Learning follow-up lessons*
Session name	*Vocabulary*	*Language structures*	*Family learning opportunity:*
1. Introduc-ing yourself & what's that in English?	Names Relevant countries Classroom vocabulary	My name is Sandra. Where do you come from? I come from. . . I don't understand. I don't know. What's that in English? It's a computer. I am the parent of. . . Articles, e.g. a/an	Introducing yourself Getting to know you ice breaker games, then show a group of items from the classroom that they learnt, e.g. pencil, paper, notebook, then hide them and take one away and show the remaining items. They need to guess what's missing. Then, hide all the items and they must try and remember all the items (work in learner and family member groups). The winning team recalls the most items.
2. Getting to know you	Pronouns, e.g. you, we, he, she, it, they Family vocabulary, e.g. mum, dad, son, daughter School staff, e.g. teacher, receptionist	How are you? I am fine, thanks. This is my (family member) I am . . . (school staff)	Introduce an adult and child Remember Book to remember new vocabulary and language structures (see Chapter 2, p. 6). Have a go at using it.
3a. Numbers and age	Counting 1–10 Counting 11–101 Classroom objects, e.g. pen, pencil, table, chair Plurals, e.g. brother, brothers, chair, chairs	How old is she/he? He is . . . years old. Verb to be 'is/are'	Counting objects in English Play some counting games, e.g. Each learner and family member have a pot with counters. They must guess how many counters in their pot and write down their number. They then count the counters in English. The winning team is the one that gets nearest the correct number of counters. Vary the items in the pots and have another go.

	A. Framework for teaching English to parents in schools (beginners)		B. Family Learning follow-up lessons
Session name	Vocabulary	Language structures	Family learning opportunity:
3b. Subject + verb + object	Basic verbs, e.g. walk, come, go, sleep, eat School vocabulary, e.g. lunch box, lost property	Third person singular Word order – Pronoun + verb, e.g. She plays with bricks.	Use the flashcards and teach the pairs game with subject + verb + object (use resources from session 9, p. 54)
4. Finding things and rooms	Possessive adjectives Rooms in a school, e.g. classroom, gym, hall, toilet Prepositional language, e.g. right, left, over there	Relative pronoun Whose. . .? E.g., Whose is this? Verb to be 'is/are,' e.g. Where is/are the . . .? It's/ They are over there/on the right.	Complete a tour of the school and use the language learnt (use resources from pre-induction session D, pp. 26-27) In pairs (learner and family member), label the room with the vocabulary on the resource sheet.
5. Talking about subjects, colours and the classroom	Colours vocabulary School subjects	Is it blue? Yes, it is./No, it isn't. Do you like History? Does your child like English? She likes English a lot.	Parents ask children subjects and colours they like. Then teach pairs (learner and family member) to use the flashcards to support English learning by playing the snap game with 'classroom and school subject vocabulary' (use resources from pre-induction sessions C, pp. 24-25 and session 3, pp. 37-40 as well as the snap; 'Collaborative games for the demonstration phase', Chapter 2, pp. 15-16).
6. Making a meeting	People in schools, e.g. teacher, teaching assistant (TA), Head-teacher Time vocabulary, e.g. clock, little hand, big hand, seconds, minutes	Can I have a meeting? (can for permission) I want to talk about. . . How is my child doing? What's the time? It's __ o'clock. It's half past. . . It's quarter past. . . It's quarter to. . . quarter past/quarter to/ o'clock/half past The meeting finishes at. . .	Telling the time together. Make a clock with a little and big hand. The parent makes a time and the learner has to tell it and vice versa.

	A. Framework for teaching English to parents in schools (beginners)		B. Family Learning follow-up lessons
Session name	Vocabulary	Language structures	Family learning opportunity:
7. Events	Special days vocabulary, e.g. Summer Holiday Days of the week Months names Ordinal number abbreviations	What day is sports day? What day does the summer holiday start? When is the holiday? It's on 27th July.	Look at the school calendar together. What days are the special events? Parent reads out a date and the child identifies it on the calendar then vice versa until they identify all the special dates on the school calendar.
8a. Your child's daily routine	Daily routine vocabulary, e.g. brushes his teeth, wake up, have a shower Time indicators, e.g. yesterday, this morning, last night Adverbs of frequency Sports vocabulary Adverbs, e.g. once, twice	Time of the day and year – in or at a time at/in, e.g. He brushes his teeth at 8am. Adverbs of frequency, daily routine and prepositions in, on, at How often does he take the bus? He takes the bus once a week.	Parents to ask children about their daily routine. Then teach pairs (learner and family member) bingo game with 'sports?' See resource session 17, pp. 79-80 and bingo; 'Collaborative games for the demonstration phase,' Chapter 2, pp. 15-16.
9. Your child's preferences	Sports/ hobbies vocabulary Food vocabulary	My child enjoys... Like and dislike vocabulary My child loves... What does your child like? Does he listen to music? Yes, he does. Do you like playing badminton? Yes, I do. Do you eat meat? No, I don't. Verb 'can/can't' for ability, e.g. He can play basketball.	How to support your child learning English through reading (about their hobbies, sports or other things of interest). Use an appropriate guided reader and the child must read to the parent. Give parents a variety of questions to ask in their home language (from those that are more literal to questions that require a learner to infer).
10. Your child's feelings	Wants and feelings vocabulary	Feelings vocabulary How are you feeling? I'm angry. He's/ She's He is . . . He wants. . ., e.g. He is bored. He wants to play. No, I don't./Yes, I do. Do you feel . . .? How was my child today? Your child was sad. How are you feeling?	Split the pairs (learner and family member) into teams. Mime the feelings for the other pair to guess. Also use resources from session 28, pp. 112-114.

	A. Framework for teaching English to parents in schools (beginners)		B. Family Learning follow-up lessons
Session name	Vocabulary	Language structures	Family learning opportunity:
11. Buying things at school	School vocabulary, e.g. shirt, school dinner, bag (Things you can buy at school)	How much is . . .? Money	Shopping experience (real or role play) Use some real money to identify amounts.
12. What does your child eat?	Food vocabulary	Determiners 'a/an/some,' e.g. a banana, some sugar Have you got a/an/any. . .? E.g. Have you got any food? Does/doesn't, e.g. My child doesn't eat. . . ' . . . because they are allergic/ religion . . .' to be taught separately	Show how to pre-learn new topics using their home language – Suggest an interesting food topic. Learners (learner and family member) should research it in their home language (maybe using the internet) then create some basic sentences on what they learnt about the topic. Children can use their parents or translators to help them produce the final sentences.
13. Class agree-ments	Class agreements vocabulary Reporting achievements Behaviour vocabulary, e.g. Playing rough	Your child must. . . Your child has received. . . Your child has received a sticker today. Past perfect, e.g. What has your child been doing? My child has been. . .	Sharing the school agreements (rules). Create an action for each of the school agreements/rules and play a mime game in teams. One person mimes the school rule and the other tries to recall it. Learner and family member then create their own home agreements in their home language that the learner and family member must adhere to at home. They can translate it into English if they wish. They can both then sign it and display it at home.
14. Body, ill-nesses and cures	Body parts vocabulary, e.g. an ankle, head, some nails Illnesses vocabulary, e.g. a cold, a sore throat	I have a/an . . ., e.g. I have a cold. Hurts, e.g. My elbow hurts. Cures vocabulary What's the matter? My knee hurts. Put a plaster on it.	Play Simon says in teams to remember parts of the body. Learner and family member must practice going to the doctors, using appropriate language for going to the doctors, e.g. Doctor: What's the matter?

	A. Framework for teaching English to parents in schools (beginners)		B. Family Learning follow-up lessons
Session name	*Vocabulary*	*Language structures*	*Family learning opportunity:*
			Patient: I have got a . . ./My . . . hurts Doctors: Put some cream on it. Then turn your classroom into a doctor's surgery with waiting chairs and a doctor. They then role play as a class.
15. Trips, travelling and other places outside the school	Types of trips vocabulary, e.g. museum, library, park Places Transport vocabulary	A trip to. . . Places vocabulary Prepositions Where is/are . . .? It is. . ./they are . . ., e.g. Where is the bicycle? It's under the bridge. Preposition 'by,' e.g. I go by bicycle.	Pre-teach the vocabulary for places. Stick some pictures of places around the room. Ask the learners to find them. Each pair must try and get all the places vocabulary before the other pairs. (Use resources from session 29, pp. 115-117)
16. School uniform	Clothes vocabulary Adjectives to describe material	How many . . .? I have. . . Which one? How many pairs of stripy socks do you have? I have three pairs of stripy socks.	Use your lost property bin to pull out items and name them. Role play asking for the items from a teacher. Create their own simple snakes and ladders game (30 spaces only with 2 snakes and 2 ladders). Every other space should have a question mark. They will need a die and two counters. Learner and family member should play against each other. Each time they land on a question mark they need to point to an item of clothes the child is wearing and say the word (if they don't remember, they can't move forward). Share an example of uniform standards. Maybe a photo showing how to wear it.

	A. Framework for teaching English to parents in schools (beginners)		B. Family Learning follow-up lessons
Session name	Vocabulary	Language structures	Family learning opportunity:
17. Maths	Calculations vocabulary Operations vocabulary, e.g. add, subtract	Preposition, e.g. before/after Asking your child to calculate – Using 'what,' e.g. 'What is . . . plus/divided by/times/minus . . .' What comes before/after 10? 9.	Ask the learner to answer the sums in their home language then in English. Give the parent an idea of what kind of Maths the child will be learning so it's appropriately pitched. Provide a number line where needed. Share some examples of standards and expectations for each year group.
18. English – writing	Basic punctuation, e.g. full stop, capital letter, comma Conjunctions	Past tense (use some various common verbs, some regular and some irregular), e.g. go/went, eat/ate, visit/visited, see/saw	Pre-teach some verbs by giving the verb then create an action. Then putting them in the past tense. Give out a previously created postcard in the simple past tense, e.g. First, we went to . . . then we saw . . . they we ate. . . . After that we. . . . The text should not have any capitals or full stops and, as a pair (learner and family member), they have to punctuate the text. They can then create their own postcards in their mother tongue and then in English. Encourage them to use their home language to help them, including translators. Share some examples of standards and expectation for each year group.
19. English – reading		Past tense continued from previous session, e.g. was/were had/have	Choose an appropriately leveled narrative book written in the past tense. Learners and parents identify the past tense verbs. Learners read to parents and the teacher provides support on how to read with their child.

Source: Across Cultures, Caroline Scott, 2018

For supporting resources, see Community Village, www.communityvillage.net

Baseline assessment

APPENDIX 1

Assessment 1

Name: _____

Date: _____

Class: _____

Survival language vocabulary/language structure assessment

Answer the questions:

1. What's your name? _____

2. How are you? _____

(session 1)

3. Write the numbers:

1   2   3   4   ____ ____ ____ ____ ____ ____ ____

____ ____ ____ ____ ____ ____ ____ ____ *21* ____ ____

____ ____ ____ ____ ____ ____ ____ ____ ____ ____

____ ____ ____ ____ ____ ____ ____ ____ ____ ____

____ ____ ____ ____ ____ ____ ____

4. How old are you? _____

(session 2)

5. What colour is this? _____

6. Is it yellow? _____

© Caroline Scott (2020), *An English as an Additional Language (EAL) Programme:*
Learning Through Images for 7–14-Year-Olds, Routledge

145

7. Is it black? _____

8. _____? Yes, it is.

9. _____? No, it isn't.

10. Label these classroom objects:

_____   _____   _____

(session 3)

11. Label these objects:

_____   _____   _____

12. Circle a or an: a / an   orange

13. Circle a or an: a / an   pen

(session 4)

14. Circle this or that:

    What's this/that in English?   What's this/that in English?

    _____   _____

    (session 5)

15. Whose _____ is this?   Whose _____ is this?   Whose _____ is this?

    _____   _____   _____

    (session 6)

16. Write the numbers:

    11   12   13   14   ____ ____ ____ ____ ____

    ____ ____ ____ ____ ____   31   ____ ____ ____ ____

    ____ ____ ____ ____ ____ ____ ____ ____ ____ ____

    ____ ____ ____ ____ ____ ____ ____ ____ ____ ____

    ____ ____ ____ ____ ____ ____ ____ ____ ____ ____

17. Circle the symbol: Multiply

    ×   −   +   ÷

18. Circle the symbol: Subtract

    ×   −   +   ÷

    (session 7)

147

19. What are these subjects?

_____   _____   _____

20. Do you like Maths? _____

21. _____ ? Yes, I do like Science.

(session 8)

22. They _____ the television.

23. She _____   He _____

(session 9)

24. Label these animals:

_____   _____   _____

25. Write down the plurals:

    Mouse = _____

    Woman = _____

    Sheep = _____

(session 10)

26. Circle this or that: Circle these or those:
    What this/that in English? What are these/those in English?

_____   _____

(session 11)

27. Label these imperatives:

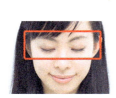      

_____   _____   _____

(session 12)

28. How many _____ and sisters has she got?

29. She has got _____.

(session 13)

Name: _____

Draw a picture of yourself ➡

Describe yourself: My name is.... I come from.... I am.... I like....

_____

_____

_____

_____

_____

_____

_____

(writing sample for independent assessment)

LearningVillage © 2018
Online English language learning for learners in schools

150

© Caroline Scott (2020), *An English as an Additional Language (EAL) Programme: Learning Through Images for 7–14-Year-Olds*, Routledge

Assessment 2

Name: _____

Date: _____

Class: _____

Survival language vocabulary/language structure assessment

Answer the questions:

1. Who is this?   Who is this?

   _____   _____

   (session 14)

2. Circle has or have: She has / have got blue eyes.

3. Circle hasn't or haven't: We hasn't / haven't got brown eyes.

4. Circle has or have:

   Has / have you got a beard?   Has / have you got brown hair?

   _____   _____

   (session 15)

5. Do you like football? Do you like cycling?

_____ _____

(session 16)

6. Can she swim? Can they surf?

_____ _____

(Session 17)

7. What is this position in the race? What is this position in the race?

He is _____ in the race. She is _____ in the race.

(Session 18)

8. What is he doing? What are they doing?

_____ _____

(Session 19)

152

© Caroline Scott (2020), *An English as an Additional Language (EAL) Programme: Learning Through Images for 7–14-Year-Olds*, Routledge

9. Circle the correct word: Have you got   *a / an / some / any* banana?

10. Circle the correct word: Have you got   *a / an / some / any* cakes?

(Session 20)

11. Circle the correct word: Yes, I have got   *a / an / some / any* apple.

12. Circle the correct word: No, I haven't got   *a / an / some / any* bottles of water.

(Session 21)

13. Circle the correct word: How *many / much* milk have you got?

14. Circle the correct word: How *many / much* biscuits have you got?

(Session 22)

15. Describe the objects and the rooms in which they are located:

There is a _____ in the _____.

There is a _____ in the _____.

There is a _____ in the _____.

16. Circle the right one:

Is there a sink in the bathroom?   **Yes, there is. / No, there isn't**   a sink in the bathroom.

(Session 23)

17. Circle the correct words:

The pen is *above / between / in* the boxes.

18. Circle the correct words:

The pen is *on top of* / *on* / *in* the box.
(Session 24)

19. Circle the correct answer:
Can I borrow your pen?

Yes, you can. / No, you can't.

20. Circle the correct answer:
Can I go to the toilet?

Yes, you can. / No, you can't.
(Session 25)

21. Circle the correct answer:
Does she dance?

Yes, I do./ No, you don't. / No, she doesn't. / Yes, she does.

22. Circle the correct question:

Does you eat meat? / Do you eat meat?

No, I don't.
(Session 26)

23. Circle the correct answer:
What would you like?

I would like some orange juice please. / I wouldn't like some orange juice please.

24. Write the correct answer:
Would you like some coffee?

_____
(Session 27)

25. Circle the correct words:

I'm happy. / I'm shy. / I'm hungry. / I'm in love.

154

© Caroline Scott (2020), *An English as an Additional Language (EAL) Programme: Learning Through Images for 7–14-Year-Olds*, Routledge

26. Circle the correct word:
    He is tired. He wants to. . .

    eat   /   sleep   /   drink   /   play

    (Session 28)

27. Name these pictures:

    _____   _____   _____

28. Circle the correct question:

    Where is the waterfall?   /   Where is the waterfalls?

    It is behind the bridge.

    (Session 29)

29. Name these directions:

       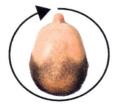   

    _____   _____   _____

    (Session 30)

LearningVillage © 2018
Online English language learning for learners in schools

Baseline assessment answers

APPENDIX 2

Assessment 1

1	What's your name? My name is...	session 1
2	How are you? I am...	session 1
3	1, 2, 3, 4, 5, 6, 7, 8, 9, 10, 11, 12, 13, 14, 15, 16, 17, 18, 19, 20	session 2
4	How old are you? I am ... years old.	session 2
5	What colour is this? This is blue.	session 3
6	Is it yellow? Yes, it is.	session 3
7	Is it black? No, it isn't.	session 3
8	Is it brown? Yes, it is.	session 3
9	Is it red? No, it isn't.	session 3
10	It is a book./It is a ruler./It is a pen.	session 3
11	It is a clock./It is a table./It is a ball.	session 4
12	an orange	session 4
13	a pen	session 4
14	What's this in English? This is a laptop. What's that in English? That's a window.	session 5
15	Whose pen is this? It's your pen./Whose backpack is this? It's my backpack./Whose apple is this? It's his apple.	session 6
16	21, 22, 23, 24, 25, 26, 27, 28, 29, 30, 31, 32, 33, 34, 35, 36, 37, 38, 39, 40	session 7
17	x	session 7
18	–	session 7
19	Maths, Science, Art	session 8
20	Do you like Maths? Yes, I do like Maths./No, I don't like Maths.	session 8
21	Do you like Science? Yes, I do like Science.	session 8
22	They watch the television.	session 9
23	She walks./He drinks.	session 9
24	These are birds./This is a horse./These are wolves.	session 10
25	Mouse = mice/woman = women/sheep = sheep	session 10
26	What's this in English?/What are these in English?	session 11
27	Close your eyes./Sit down./Open the door.	session 12
28	How many brothers and sisters has she got?	session 13
29	She has got __ brothers and sisters.	session 13

157

	Assessment 2	
1	Who is this? This is her father./This is his grandfather.	session 14
2	She has got blue eyes.	session 15
3	We haven't got brown eyes.	session 15
4	Have you got a beard?/Have you got brown hair?	session 15
5	Do you like football? Yes, I do./No, I don't. Do you like cycling? Yes, I do./No, I don't.	session 16
6	Can she swim? Yes, she can swim./Can they surf? No, they can't surf.	session 17
7	What is this position in the race? He is fourth in the race./She is sixth in the race.	session 18
8	What is he doing? He is playing the guitar. What are they doing? They are going to the cinema.	session 19
9	Have you got a banana?	session 20
10	Have you got any cakes?	session 20
11	Yes, I have got an apple.	session 21
12	No, I haven't got any bottles of water.	session 21
13	How much milk have you got?	session 22
14	How many biscuits have you got?	session 22
15	There is a spoon in the kitchen. There is a bed in the bedroom. There is a bath tub in the bathroom.	session 23
16	Is there a sink in the bathroom? Yes, there is a sink in the bathroom.	session 23
17	The pen is between the boxes.	session 24
18	The pen is in the box.	session 24
19	Can I borrow your pen? No, you can't.	session 25
20	Can I go to the toilet? Yes, you can.	session 25
21	Does she dance? No, she doesn't.	session 26
22	Do you eat meat? No, I don't.	session 26
23	What would you like? I would like some orange juice please.	session 27
24	Would you like some coffee? No, I wouldn't, thank you.	session 27
25	I'm shy.	session 28
26	He is tired. He wants to sleep.	session 28
27	Cinema/train station/shop	session 29
28	Where is the waterfall? It is behind the bridge.	session 29
29	Turn left./Turn around./Go straight on.	session 30

Assessment for learning forms

APPENDIX 3

Assessment for learning form   Pupil name and understanding ρ(see assessment chapter))

The pupil can successfully: Names:						Notes for future planning
Vocabulary – introductions **Language structure** – What's your name? My name is. . ./How are you? She is. . . **Assessed in:** assessment 1, questions 1–2 (Session 1)						
Vocabulary – numbers 1–20 **Language structure** – How old are you? I am . . . years old. **Assessed in:** assessment 1, questions 3–4 (Session 2)						
Vocabulary – colours, classroom **Language structure** – Is it. . .? Yes, it is./ No, it isn't. **Assessed in:** assessment 1, questions 5–10 (Session 3)						
Vocabulary – classroom instructions, vowels **Language structure** – a/an **Assessed in:** assessment 1, questions 11–13 (Session 4)						
Language structure – What's this/that? It's a/an. . . **Assessed in:** assessment 1, question 14 (Session 5)						
Vocabulary – possessive adjectives (his, hers, yours, my) **Language structure** – Whose is this/that? It's. . . **Assessed in:** assessment 1, question 15 (Session 6)						

© Caroline Scott (2020), *An English as an Additional Language (EAL) Programme: Learning Through Images for 7–14-Year-Olds*, Routledge

The pupil can successfully: Names:					Notes for future planning
Vocabulary – numbers, calculations **Assessed in:** assessment 1, questions 16–18 (Session 7)					
Vocabulary – levels of like, subjects **Language structure** – Do you like...? **Assessed in:** assessment 1, questions 19–21 (Session 8)					
Vocabulary – verbs **Language structure** – pronoun + verb, word order **Assessed in:** assessment 1, questions 22–23 (Session 9)					
Vocabulary – animals **Language structure** – This is a/an..., (irregular) plurals **Assessed in:** assessment 1, questions 23–25 (Session 10)					
Language structure – What are these? There are... **Assessed in:** assessment 1, question 26 (Session 11)					
Language structure – Imperatives **Assessed in:** assessment 1, question 27 (Session 12)					
Vocabulary – family **Language structure** – How many brothers and sisters has he/she got? He/she has got... **Assessed in:** assessment 1, questions 28–29 (Session 13)					
Vocabulary – family **Language structure** – Who is this? This is... **Assessed in:** assessment 2, question 1 (Session 14)					
Vocabulary – descriptions/attributes **Language structure** – He has got... **Assessed in:** assessment 2, questions 2–4 (Session 15)					
Vocabulary – sports **Language structure** – Do you like...? Yes, I do./No, I don't. **Assessed in:** assessment 2, question 5 (Session 16)					

© Caroline Scott (2020), *An English as an Additional Language (EAL) Programme: Learning Through Images for 7–14-Year-Olds*, Routledge

The pupil can successfully: Names:					Notes for future planning
Vocabulary – sports **Language structure** – He can… **Assessed in:** assessment 2, question 6 (Session 17)					
Vocabulary – ordinals 1st – 10th **Assessed in:** assessment 2, question 7 (Session 18)					
Vocabulary – hobbies **Assessed in:** assessment 2, question 8 (Session 19)					
Vocabulary – food **Language structure** – Do you have…? Yes, I have got… **Assessed in:** assessment 2, questions 9–10 (Session 20)					
Language structure – I have/haven't got a/an/some… **Assessed in:** assessment 2, questions 11–12 (Session 21)					
Vocabulary – food **Language structure** – How much/many … have you got? **Assessed in:** assessment 2, questions 13–14 (Session 22)					
Vocabulary – rooms of the house, home **Language structure** – There is/are …, There isn't/aren't … **Assessed in:** assessment 2, questions 15–16 (Session 23)					
Language structure – There is/are a/an/some… **Assessed in:** assessment 2, questions 17–18 (Session 24)					
Language structure – Can I …? Yes, you can./No, you can't. **Assessed in:** assessment 2, questions 19–20 (Session 25)					
Language structure – Do you …?/Does he …? No, I don't./Yes, he does. **Assessed in:** assessment 2, questions 21–22 (Session 26)					

The pupil can successfully: Names:					*Notes for future planning*
Vocabulary – food and drinks **Language structure** – What would you like? I would like …, Would you like …? Yes, I would./No, I wouldn't thank you. **Assessed in:** assessment 2, questions 23–24 (Session 27)					
Vocabulary – wants and feelings **Language structure** – He is …, She wants to… **Assessed in:** assessment 2, questions 25–26 (Session 28)					
Vocabulary – places **Language** structure – Where is/are …? It is… **Assessed in:** assessment 2, questions 27–28 (Session 29)					
Vocabulary – directions **Language structure** – Where is …? **Assessed in:** assessment 2, question 29 (Session 30)					

EAL assessment continuum

APPENDIX 4

The Bell Foundation highlights:

"The Bell Foundation's EAL Assessment Framework for Schools is the first and only theoretically and empirically informed framework which is freely available to all schools and other stakeholders in England. It provides teachers with an academically robust, curriculum-based, easy-to-use framework for assessing the language proficiency of pupils with English as an Additional Language.

The Framework was developed by a team of top academics and EAL professionals including Professor Constant Leung, King's College London; Dr. Michael Evans and Dr. Yongcan Liu, Cambridge University and Dr. Neil Jones, Language Consultant, formerly Cambridge English Language Assessment. It was developed with the aim of supporting teachers working with over one million EAL pupils in primary and secondary schools.

The framework forms part of The Bell Foundation's EAL programme. The Bell Foundation is a UK-based charity whose main aim is to overcome exclusion through language education by working with partners on innovation, research, training and practical interventions.

The assessment descriptors within the framework form two sets of rating scales – one for Primary and one for Secondary. Each of set of scales covers the four strands of language knowledge and use: Listening, Speaking, Reading and Viewing and Writing.

English language Proficiency in each strand is represented by five Proficiency bands and each band has a descriptive label:

A-New to English/Beginning
B-Early acquisition/Emerging
C-Developing competence/Expanding
D-Competent/Diversifying
E-Fluent.

Each band within the Framework has 10 internal assessment descriptors. Pupils are not expected to achieve all the descriptors within a band and it is likely that some pupils attain the descriptors in a different order to those listed; this is not unusual and is not a cause for concern. However, it is important to be aware that the descriptors are sequenced to reflect internal progression within each band of descriptors, e.g. descriptors 1–3 are 'early development' and descriptors 8–10 are 'getting closer to the next band'. Although the descriptors are not expected to be achieved in strict order by all pupils, this way of ordering the descriptors within each band enables teachers to set targets from the descriptors and to track progression.

At the core of the framework are the EAL assessment descriptors that teachers can use for both summative and formative assessment. The descriptors are designed specifically to support the teaching and learning of EAL pupils and to enable teachers to generate targets to guide progress.

The framework includes a set of classroom support strategies which map directly onto the relevant individual descriptors within the framework and provides highly practical ways to support EAL learners at each stage of their language development. There are also guiding principles and strategies for practitioners working with learners who use EAL in EYFS settings.

The EAL Assessment Framework for Schools, classroom support strategies and guiding principles for practitioners working with EAL learners in EYFS will be updated from time to time. To download the complete framework, you should visit The Bell Foundation website at www.bell-foundation.org.uk.

PRIMARY
READING & VIEWING

Name: Class: First Language:

CODE	Band A — Showing little or no knowledge of written English; taking first steps to engage with written and digital texts in English	Band B — Making sense of written text at word and phrase/sentence level, using visual information to help decipher meaning	Band C — Drawing on growing knowledge of vocabulary and grammar to engage with curriculum-related texts and tasks	Band D — Working with written language and accompanying visuals productively, using different strategies in response to curriculum tasks	Band E — Engaging with curriculum-related reading activities independently and productively in different subject areas
1 (Early Development)	Can make use of their cultural and linguistic experiences to try to make sense of words in digital and print forms (i.e. doesn't understand but can distinguish between words and numbers or symbols or text types - advertisement or newspaper article)	Can recognise words and the sequences of words that form familiar phrases or expressions (e.g. 'once upon a time')	Can recognise and read irregular (but frequently occurring) spelling patterns (e.g. '-tre' in 'centre')	Can relate written material to classroom activities and understand that written material is often organised and presented differently from spoken language (e.g. written instructions for science experiments versus teacher and peer talk while conducting the experiment)	Can process information in written texts that are structured differently from that gained through spoken language, even if they are on the same topic or have similar content
2	Can follow written text conventions (e.g. left to right movement (in English), continuity of text from top to bottom of page)	Can use awareness of grapheme-phoneme correspondence to try to decode unfamiliar words/phrases	Can recognise common prefixes (e.g. 're' in 'return') and suffixes (e.g. 'ed' in 'walked') and punctuation, and use this awareness and knowledge to make sense of text	Can identify the purpose and intended audience of curriculum-related texts without prompting	Can understand and interpret visuals and graphics in conjunction with written text appropriately
3	Can understand that written text and visuals have content, meaning and organisation (e.g. front and back covers of a book)	Can attempt to work with familiar and some unfamiliar words in phrases/sentences, and try to make sense of them	Can make sense of curriculum texts but may need support to comprehend unfamiliar content, culturally engendered nuances (e.g. 'the angel twinkled on the top of the tree'), and figurative and metaphoric expressions (e.g. 'don't wind him up', 'life is a roller coaster')	Can recognise meaning of words/phrases expressing degrees of obligation, probability and possibility in context (e.g. may, must, should)	Can understand the meaning - such as identifying the agent when not obvious and the sequence of happenings - contained in sentences and passages based on knowledge of more complex grammar (e.g. the passive voice 'No pocket money until you tidy your room. You have been warned,' said Mum)
4	Can distinguish and understand different forms of meaning representation, (e.g. letters, words, visual images and graphics)	Can use own growing language knowledge to process text at the phrase/sentence level, showing awareness of idiomatic expressions, (e.g. 'in the beginning', 'a long time ago')	Can identify and interpret information from visual images, tables, charts and graphs, and relate it to the task at hand	Can use growing knowledge of grammar to try to make sense of complex expressions (e.g. conditional constructions such as 'If I had a choice … I would …')	Can recognise complex cohesive markers to link ideas across sentences and passages (e.g. although, in spite of, pronouns referring back across several sentences e.g. 'The stone age was … It …')
5 (not expected to be achieved in order)	Can recognise names, including own name, and labels of objects and spaces in the classroom and other familiar parts of the school (e.g. school office)	Can comprehend taught/rehearsed short written passages at whole-text level, using visuals as support where appropriate	Can identify main ideas in curriculum material and use own prior experience and learning to assist understanding where appropriate	Can follow written material to do tasks such as classifying and sequencing events in narratives, descriptions and processes in subject content texts independently	Can find specific information or detail from written texts to respond to 'how', 'who' or 'why' questions
6	Can match pictures and other visuals with taught/rehearsed words	Can attempt to read/check own writing for meaning with teacher/peer support	Can understand most subject content texts, including factual accounts, narratives, opinion pieces; although may need support with unfamiliar vocabulary, complex sentences and writing styles	Can identify figurative speech (e.g. 'a star was born') and metaphoric expressions (e.g. 'he bottled up his anger') in curriculum texts (and seek help if necessary)	Can identify explicit and implicit messages in informational and fictional texts
7	Can make sense of familiar words in books, on signs and posters in school and in frequently visited digital environments	Can identify and extract information (words and passages) in texts in response to concrete what, where and who questions	Can comprehend curriculum-linked English literature mostly at the literal level, but may rely on teacher and peer support to understand cultural references and meanings	Can recognise different text types/genres, understanding that the purpose of communication can shape text organisation (e.g. a narrative of personal experience versus a report of a science experiment)	Can evaluate an informational or fictional text in terms of its interest, relevance and usefulness
8	Can recognise and use sound-symbol correspondence to decipher the meaning of some words in a taught/rehearsed text	Can read out loud short texts with familiar/predictable structures written in everyday languages, attempting to use pauses and intonation to mark meaning	Can retrieve relevant details from curriculum and literary texts to retell the gist of content	Can use a developing range of reading strategies, especially when prompted (e.g. adjusting their reading rate for the task at hand), using dictionaries or other references	Can draw own conclusion/form own opinion from reading where appropriate (e.g. when participating in class and group discussions)
9	Can follow and make use of familiar words to extract basic meaning from a familiar text	Can begin to work out main points, story lines and explicit messages from illustrated text without prompting	Can begin to differentiate between informational and fictional statements/texts independently	Can reread a text to check understanding if told that the information in the text has not been completely understood	Can analyse curriculum-related texts in terms of nature/type of content, organisation and purpose
10 (Getting Closer to the Next Band)	Can choose books or other reading materials to join in learning activities, especially when guided	Can use growing awareness of familiar grapheme-phoneme correspondence, spelling patterns, and contextual clues to work out the meaning of unfamiliar words, phrases and short texts	Can use compositional and design features of print and digital material to navigate and locate information (e.g. contents pages, links, tabs, search functions)	Can identify main ideas and specific information in curriculum-related texts for retelling, paraphrasing and answering questions	Can independently apply reading skills and strategies already acquired to engage with new texts at word, sentence, and whole-text levels, using visuals and prior knowledge to enhance understanding

Copyright © The Bell Educational Trust Limited (operating as The Bell Foundation) September 2017, Version 1.1

© Caroline Scott (2020), *An English as an Additional Language (EAL) Programme: Learning Through Images for 7–14-Year-Olds*, Routledge

PRIMARY WRITING

Name: Class: First Language:

CODE	Band A — Showing attempts at writing in English	Band B — Demonstrating basic skills of spelling and sentence construction	Band C — Demonstrating competence in independent use of vocabulary and construction of simple sentences	Band D — Demonstrating competence in independent use of diverse vocabulary, sentences and genres with increased accuracy and fluency	Band E — Demonstrating enhanced ability in writing with greater accuracy and for a variety of purposes, mostly at age-expected level
1 (Early Development)	Can mark/indicate familiar pictures, numbers and other visual images	Can show awareness of common and simple spelling rules (e.g. can show awareness of basic phonics and starting to spell common consonant-vowel-consonant (CVC) words correctly, such as 'hat', 'ant', 'sit')	Can use appropriate time sequencing (e.g. 'first', 'next', 'finally')	Can employ a range of modal elements (e.g. 'would', 'should', 'could', 'might') and tenses (including present continuous tense, simple past tense) to construct a text	Can demonstrate full control over grammatical features (including types of verb, pronoun reference, compound and complex sentences)
2	Can communicate intentions and own meaning through drawing and mark making	Can form and reproduce most English letters and attempt to produce words	Can attempt to construct a coherent sentence with familiar vocabulary, including common articles (e.g. 'a', 'the'), prepositions (e.g. 'on', 'in') and conjunctions (e.g. 'and', 'but')	Can identify spelling errors in words used in curriculum subjects when proofreading their own writing	Can write in clear, well-structured English across the curriculum using appropriate style and layout
3	Can show awareness of the differences between print and picture in attempting to write	Can jot down a phrase/sentence from audio/video material and orally rehearse it by themselves	Can use some formulaic expressions in writing (e.g. 'excuse me', 'I suppose so', 'at the beginning', 'once upon a time')	Can combine phrases/sentences to produce a clear and coherent statement in relation to curriculum tasks	Can use a variety of tenses (including present and past perfect)
4	Can show awareness of some basic conventions of writing (e.g. writing from left to right – significant if this is not the convention in the pupil's first language; leaving spaces between symbols or letters)	Can complete sentence starters if examples are provided (e.g. 'I like [apples]', 'The monkey ate [four bananas]')	Can use some grammatical structures, such as subject-verb agreement (e.g. 'he walks'), inflections (e.g. adding 'ed' to form the past tense)	Can write grammatical sentences on familiar topics (e.g. meeting friends, participating in sports events)	Can write competently for a range of classroom purposes
5 (not expected to be achieved in order)	Can form and reproduce some English letters	Can follow examples and reproduce taught expectations about layout (e.g. front cover, page number)	Can produce longer sentences based on familiar taught content, but writing reflects features of spoken language (e.g. 'Yesterday, I ..., then I went home')	Can write stories and descriptions of personal experience in an appropriate time sequence	Can connect or integrate personal experiences with literary writing
6	Can copy or write own name	Can make independent use of basic punctuations to achieve various purposes (e.g. using commas to separate ideas, capitals to start a sentence)	Can combine ideas based on taught content, although they are not fully accurate (e.g. 'stone age peoples use sharp stone')	Can use text models to scaffold content and structure of writing for different classroom purposes	Can express ideas and opinions effectively for expectations of age group
7	Can use first language to scaffold their effort to form English words (e.g. words from other languages used in English, such as French 'table')	Can copy passages from an English text in the curriculum (significant if the pupil's first language is in a different script)	Can show understanding of content of taught sessions through writing using familiar vocabulary and sentence models	Can begin to use phrases/sentences in a culturally-appropriate way in different areas of the curriculum	Can write reports using technical vocabulary (e.g. scientific experiments)
8	Can start to write English to fill in blanks, copy known words or label diagrams/images (e.g. labelling a map)	Can combine drawing and writing to create meaningful sentences on familiar topics (e.g. a picture of a house with 'This is my home')	Can draw on first language to plan writing (e.g. use words from first language to scaffold ideas)	Can compare, contrast and summarise content-based information (e.g. environment, education)	Can justify, defend and debate opinions based on supporting information and evidence
9	Can contribute to a shared story in the class and produce letters and strings of letters associated with pictures	Can form simple sentences using word/phrase banks for different classroom purposes (e.g. words and phrases highlighted in curriculum tasks)	Can construct simple connected text based on short descriptions of events and activities for classroom purposes	Can participate in shared writing activities or write independently	Can plan writing with a particular audience in mind (e.g. letter of complaint, persuasive leaflet)
10 (Getting Closer to the Next Band)	Can copy/reproduce letters shown by teachers to make their own meaning when telling a story	Can write some simple basic phrases or sentences in relation to personal experience (e.g. family, home, playground activities)	Can attempt to write short texts in different genres (e.g. first person diary entry, letter, third person narrative)	Can produce texts in a variety of genres (e.g. narrative, argumentation, description) using subject- or topic-related vocabulary	Can review, revise and edit work with teachers or independently (depending on age)

Each cell includes Autumn / Spring / Summer checkboxes and Academic Year field.

Copyright © The Bell Educational Trust Limited (operating as The Bell Foundation) September 2017, Version 1.1

NASSEA English as an Additional Language (EAL) Assessment Framework

© Caroline Scott (2020), *An English as an Additional Language (EAL) Programme: Learning Through Images for 7–14-Year-Olds*, Routledge

NASSEA states

"The Framework is a cross-curricular tool which helps practitioners to observe, document and accelerate the ways bilingual pupils start to use English as a tool for learning in school, then continue to develop their use of English through all their subject areas.

It describes the development of communicative behaviour in class and language for learning through listening, speaking, reading and writing. It also includes some aspects of personal development likely to be significant for bilingual learners, such as readiness to speak to others in the classroom.

It is important to note that the framework is not a tool to be used to assess other languages the pupil may speak. NASSEA supports the continuing use and development of pupils' other languages, and reference is made to using skills in these languages, but this tool is only for assessing English as an Additional Language.

The Framework has been developed to help practitioners to become more aware of the progress of their EAL learners through formative assessment.

NASSEA EAL Assessment Framework Overview

Copyright NASSEA 2015

	Step 1 Surviving a school day	Step 2 Reacting to learning experiences	Step 3 Engaging more independently	Step 4 Emerging control over language tools	Step 5 Developing fuller understanding, extending responses	Step 6 TRANSITION	Step 7 The need for support reduces	Step 8 Fluency, monitoring
Listening/ Understanding	Can understand classroom words. Can respond to one step instructions. Can learn and use new words taught in class.	Can understand one-step, familiar, practical and short speech.	Can use scaffolding, support and differentiation provided in class. Can understand targets and appropriate learning objectives. Can pick up and use new vocabulary quickly.	Can understand beyond the simplest part of the lesson.	Can understand the gist of a lesson at normal pace. Can deal with routine events in school.	*The pupil can sometimes perform close to age-appropriate expectations. The pupil will sometimes perform at a much lower standard than was expected. This is because the pupil's need for contextual support is greater under some circumstances. Providing more contextual support at times of change and the bat the start of a new unit of work will raise attainment.*	Can understand the gist of the lesson with no adjustment for EAL. Can interact spontaneously during all class activities.	Can understand the content of a lesson in the same way as most peers.
Speaking	Can answer where, what, who, when questions. Can produce learned words, learned short phrases. Can communicate with people who adjust the conversation for EAL needs.	Can communicate about the concrete, the practical and the familiar. Can retell short and simple content delivered supportively. Can speak in longer phrases and sentences with scaffolding.	Can ask for clarification in a focussed way. Can speak independently in longer, communicative utterances. Can express a lot of lesson content.	Can express content independently. Can be easily understood. Can express content very well with scaffolding and rehearsal.	Can converse socially and on task. Can communicate familiar content and own observations with detail. Can describe, narrate and share reasoning and opinions, although with errors.		Can converse about lesson content with only minor errors. Can express both concrete and abstract ideas. Can explain own reasoning.	Can use English spontaneously in an age appropriate way. Can use English effectively, both socially and academically.
Reading	Can read own name. Can understand signage in school. Can understand labels. Can recognise words by shape and first letter.	Can answer one-step who, what, where, when questions relating to text. Can read simple text relating to something already discussed. Can locate high content words in texts. Can recognise most initial consonants.	Can locate taught features of text and layout. Can retrieve information at a simple level. Can read with understanding a differentiated text. Can use phonic skills.	Can attempt a range of texts. Can decode unfamiliar words. Can retell text content with scaffolding.	Can understand a simple text, if the vocabulary is mostly familiar.		Can read an age-appropriate text and understand the main points.	Can understand age-appropriate texts. Can understand inference at an age-appropriate level.
Writing	Can form most letters. Can copy known words. Can conform to taught layout.	Can write short sentences with scaffolding. Can attempt some independent writing. Can use capital letters and full stops.	Can write sentences about familiar content. Can use a model to improve writing. Can produce easily read handwriting. Can use more taught punctuation.	Can write meaningful sentences and short text with scaffolding. Can use common spelling patterns. Can use basic punctuation independently. Can apply common spelling patterns.	Can write a simple paragraph about familiar content.		Can write clearly, with details. Can explain own point of view, giving reasons. Can explain advantages and disadvantages.	Can produce detailed, well-structured, cohesive texts at an age-appropriate level.
	Short phrases, single words.	Can recognise that verbs change form, but cannot yet use verb forms with accuracy	Can use more grammatical features, adopting what s/he hears others say, but with errors. Uses 'and' 'because'.	Can self-correct some grammatical mistakes.	Can communicate in cohesive English, although with errors.		Can use features of grammar associated with higher order thinking skills, if these have been taught and modelled.	Unfamiliarity with some aspects of the language, or with some vocabulary, can cause underachievement if teachers are not aware of the pupil's language needs.

© Caroline Scott (2020), *An English as an Additional Language (EAL) Programme: Learning Through Images for 7–14-Year-Olds*, Routledge

167

APPENDIX 5

Small-group support record

Learners	Date	Lesson/s	Outcome	Other comments

© Caroline Scott (2020), *An English as an Additional Language (EAL) Programme: Learning Through Images for 7–14-Year-Olds*, Routledge

Glossary

Adjective

A word that describes somebody or something. It describes a noun. It normally comes before a noun, e.g. *big* horse or *blue* car.

Adverb

A word that describes a verb.

Article

This is a type of determiner (a class of words occurring before a noun). There is a definite article which is 'the' or the indefinite article which are 'a' and 'an.'

Apostrophe

The symbol ('). 1. Used to indicate missing letters, e.g. I've. 2. Used to indicate possession, e.g. The girl's socks – the apostrophe is placed before the s. When the noun is plural already, the apostrophe is placed after the s, e.g. The girls' socks.

Baseline assessment

To assess what a learner already knows and can do on entering a school. A non-graded test is used for this.

Cardinal number

A number, e.g. one, two, three.

Clause A section of a sentence that contains a subject and a verb.

Countable noun

A noun that has both a plural and a singular form, e.g. a pig, two pigs.

Comprehensible input

This term is used to refer to language that is intelligible but may be more advanced than the student's current ability to understand it. This commonly happens when an intermediate English learner is immersed in the English-speaking mainstream. It means the main message of the language is understood even though some words and language structures might be unfamiliar. This term comes from Stephen Krashen's theory of second language acquisition.

Determiner

A group of words that fall before the noun, e.g. a, an, some, this, the.

ESOL classes

English to Speaking of Other Languages (ESOL) usually refers to adult English language classes.

Formative assessment

This indicates stages reached, which then helps to identify areas of subsequent work and development.

Graphic organizer

Graphic organizer's purpose is to form a supportive structure for organizing and generating ideas, which serves as a preparation for later independence. For example, we can have comparison graphic organizers which help us compare our ideas.

High frequency words

The most used words. These words are therefore very useful to the learner.

High order thinking skills

Some types of learning require more cognitive processing than others and we need to develop across learning that encompasses a range. For example, knowledge and comprehension would be low order thinking skills, yet analysis, synthesis and evaluation would be high order thinking skills. It is thought that different levels of thinking require different types of teaching methodology. It is based on Bloom's taxonomy.

Language form

The grammatical structure of words (language structure) and phrases as well as the vocabulary (words) themselves. For example, descriptive adjectives, past tense verbs or sentence structure using modals, e.g. will, may.

Language function

What learners do with language as they engage and converse with it. The function results in the use of language for a specific purpose. For example, comparing or evaluating.

Infinitive

The basic form of a verb, e.g. to see, to sleep.

Kinaesthetic

A word used to describe activities that involve bodily movement. Kinaesthetic learners need to learn by doing.

New arrival

In this case, a pupil new to a school who speaks little or no English.

Noun

A word used to refer to somebody or something. A noun includes names of people, animals, objects, substances, events and feelings. Nouns can be divided into two groups: countable and uncountable.

Object

A noun or pronoun that normally comes after the verb in a clause containing an action verb, e.g. break, told. In 'Trish sees the dog,' 'Trish' is the subject and 'the dog' is the object.

Ordinal number

A number defining a noun's position, e.g. first, second, third.

Plural

More than one.

Possessive adjective

These are determiners such as my, her, his, its, their, our, your.

Pronoun

A noun used instead of the name of someone who is already mentioned, e.g. he, she, this.

Punctuation

Marks that help readers interpret text.

Scaffolding

A process a teacher uses to model or demonstrate how to solve a problem (in the case of language learning, to support learners with using the language needed to articulate themselves). After modelling, they step back, offering support as needed.

Sentence

A complete set of words that have meaning. Sentences normally have one or more clauses and usually at least one subject and verb. A simple sentence is a sentence with one clause only, e.g. I was early.

Singular

Only one of something.

Subject

The subject is the 'what' or 'who' that the sentence is about.

Syllable

The beat of a word, e.g. el – e – phant.

Tense

A word used to describe time of action, happening or process highlighted by the verb, e.g. past – went, present – go and future – will go.

Third person

Used to talk about a third party, e.g. he, she.

Uncountable noun

For example, water, milk, wood or air. These nouns usually have no plural forms.

Verb

A word used to describe an action, state or occurrence. Often described as a 'doing' or 'being' word, e.g. shout, become.

Vocabulary

Words used for specific language, e.g. transport vocabulary.

Vowel

The five vowels are a, e, i, o, u. Every syllable contains a vowel sound.

Abbreviations

EAL – English as an Additional Language

ESOL – English to Speak of Other Languages

ICT – Information Communication Technology

TA – Teaching Assistant

Bibliography

Beaumont, D. (1993) *Elementary English Grammar: An Elementary Reference and Practice Book*, Basingstoke, UK: Macmillan Heinemann

Black, P. and William, D. (1998a) Assessment and classroom learning, *Assessment in Education*, 5(1), 7–74

Black, P. and William, D. (1998b) *Inside the Black Box: Raising Standards Through Classroom Assessment*, London: King's College School of Education

Brown, N. and Chadfield, S. (2014) *Writing It Right*, London: Borough Tower Hamlets

Carrasquillo, A., Kucer, S. and Abrams, R. (2004) *Beyond the Beginnings: Literacy Interventions for Upper Elementary English Language Learners*, Bristol, UK: Multilingual Matters

Carrasquillo, A. and Rodriguez, V. (2002) *Language Minority Students in the Mainstream*, Bristol, UK: Multilingual Matters

Clarke, S. (2001) *Unlocking Formative Assessment: Practical Strategies for Enhancing Pupils' Learning in the Primary Classroom*, London: Hodder & Stoughton

Creese, A. (2005) *Teacher Collaboration and Talk in Multilingual Classrooms*, Toronto, Canada: Multilingual Matters

Cummins, J. (1994) *Negotiating Identities: Education for Empowerment in a Diverse Society*, Los Angeles, CA: California Association for Bilingual Education

Cummins, J. (2000) *Language, Power and Pedagogy: Bilingual Children in the Crossfire*. Bristol, UK: Multilingual Matters

Department for Education. (2014) *National Curriculum in England: Framework Document for Teaching*, London, https://www.gov.uk/government/publications/national-curriculum-in-england-framework-for-key-stages-1-to-4/the-national-curriculum-in-england-framework-for-key-stages-1-to-4

Department for Education. (2015) *Education Data Division – Request for Change Form for CBDS*, https://assets.publishing.service.gov.uk/government/uploads/system/uploads/attachment_data/file/509299/RFC_875_-_new_data_item_for_proficiency_in_English.pdf, accessed 22nd July 2018

Driver, J. (2018) *Assistant Principal, at Queen Katherine Academy, ESOL Is Not a Dirty Word!* Speaker at Language Show Live 2018, London

Echevarría, J. (2012) *Effective Practices for Increasing the Achievement of English Learners*, Long Beach, CA: California State University, www.cal.org/create, accessed 26th July 2018

Echevarria, J. and Graves, A. (2010) *Sheltered Content Instruction: Teaching Students with Diverse Abilities*, Fourth Edition, Boston, MA: Allyn & Bacon

Echevarria, J. and Short, D. (2010) Programs and practices for effective sheltered content instruction. In California Department of Education (Ed.), *Improving Education for English Learners: Research-Based Approaches*, Sacramento, CA: California Department of Education Press

Echevarria, J., Vogt, M. and Short, D. (2013) *Making Content Comprehensible for English Learners, The SIOP Model*, London: Pearson

Gallagher, E. (2008) *Equal Rights to the Curriculum*, Bristol, UK: Multilingual Matters

Genesee, F., Savage, R., Erdos, C. and Haigh, C. (2013) Identification of reading difficulties in students schooled in a second language. In V. C. M. Gathercole (Ed.), *Solutions for Assessment of Bilinguals*, Bristol, UK: Multilingual Matters

Gibbons, P. (2009) *English Learners Academic Literacy and Thinking*, Portsmouth, New Hampshire: Heinemann

Gu, Y. (2010) *Advance Review: A New Book on Teaching and Researching Language Learning Strategies*. Unpublished review, Wellington University, NZ

Hutchinson, J. (2018) *Educational Outcomes of Children with English as an Additional Language*, London: Bell Foundation, Education Policy Institute, https://epi.org.uk/wp-content/uploads/2018/02/EAL_Educational-Outcomes_EPI-1.pdf, accessed 14th February 2018

Hwang, W-Y., Shih, T. K., Yeh, S-C., Chou, K-C., Ma, Z-H. and Sommool, W. (2014) Recognition-based physical response to facilitate EFL learning, *Educational Technology & Society*, 17(4), 432–445

Integrated Communities English Language Programme. (2018) *Integrated Communities English Language Programme: Prospectus,* https://www.gov.uk/government/publications/integrated-communities-english-language-programme-prospectus

Kareva, V. and Echevarria, J. (2013) *Using the SIOP Model for Effective Content Teaching with Second and Foreign*

Language Learners, Long Beach, CA: California State University

Lightbrown, P. M. and Spada, N. (2013) *How Languages Are Learned (Oxford Handbooks for Language Teachers)*. Oxford: Oxford University Press

Lileikienė, A. and Danilevičienė, L. (2016) Foreign language anxiety in student learning, *Baltic Journal of Sport & Health Sciences*, 3(102), 18–23, Lithuanian Sports University, Kaunas, Lithuania

Lombardi, J. (2008) Beyond learning styles: Brain-based research and English language learners, *Clearing House: A Journal of Educational Strategies, Issues and Ideas*, 81(5), May-June, 219–222

López-Vargas, O., Ibáñez-Ibáñez, J. and Racines-Prada, O. (2017) Students' metacognition and cognitive style and their effect on cognitive load and learning achievement, *Educational Technology & Society*, 20(3), 145–157

Mohan, B., Leung, C. and Davison, C. (2001) *English as a Second Language in the Mainstream: Teaching, Learning and Identity*

Murphy, R. (1998) *Essential Grammar in Use*, Cambridge, UK: Cambridge University Press

Murphy, R. (2006a) *Essential Grammar in Use, a Self-Study Reference and Practice Book for Elementary Students of English, Cambridge*, Cambridge, UK: Cambridge University Press

Murphy, R. (2006b) *Essential Grammar in Use, a Self-Study Reference and Practice Book for Intermediate Learners of English, Cambridge*, Cambridge, UK: Cambridge University Press

NASSEA. (2016) *EAL Assessment Framework, Curriculum and Language Access Service*, www.nassea.org.uk/eal-assessment-framework/

Nation, P. and Waring, R. (1997) Vocabulary size, text coverage and word lists. In N. Schmitt and M. McCarthy (Eds.), *Vocabulary, Description, Acquisition and Pedagogy*, Cambridge, UK: Cambridge University Press

National Curriculum of England. (2014) *National Curriculum in England: Framework for Key Stages 1 to 4,* https://www.gov.uk/government/publications/national-curriculum-in-england-framework-for-key-stages-1-to-4/the-national-curriculum-in-england-framework-for-key-stages-1-to-4

National Curriculum of England. (2014) *The National Curriculum in England: Key Stages 1 and 2 Framework Document.* © Crown copyright 2013. www.gov.uk/dfe/nationalcurriculum

National Learning and Work Institute. (2018) *Measuring the Impact of Community-Based English Language Provision: Findings from a Randomised Controlled Trial*, London: Ministry of Housing, Communities and Local Government

Norbert, S. and McCarthy, M. (1998) *Vocabulary: Description, Acquisition and Pedagogy*, Cambridge, UK: Cambridge University Press

Pedaste, M., Mäeots, M., Siiman, L. A., De Jong, T., van Riesen, S. A. N., Kamp, E. T., Manoli, C. C., Zacharia, Z. C. and Tsourlidaki, E. (2015) Phases of inquiry-based learning: Definitions and inquiry cycle, *Educational Research Review*, 14, 47–61

Redman, S. (2013) *English Vocabulary in Use, Pre-intermediate & Intermediate*, Cambridge, UK: Cambridge University Press

Rieser, S., Naumann, A., Decristan, J., Fauth, B., Klieme, E. and Buttner, G. (2016) The connection between teaching and learning: Linking teaching quality and metacognitive strategy use in primary school, *British Journal of Educational Psychology*, 86, 526–545

Rose, J. (2006) *Independent Review of the Teaching of Early Reading*, Nottingham: Department for Education and Skills

Scott, C. (2007) *Teaching Children English as an Additional Language: A Programme for 7–11 Year Olds*, Milton, OX: Routledge

Scott, C. (2012) *Teaching English as an Additional Language 5–11: A Whole School Resource*, Milton, OX: Routledge

Scott, C. (2016) *How You Can Support Students' Mother Tongue Development*, Suffolk, UK: International Schools Magazine, John Catt Educational Ltd

Sears, C. (2015) *Second Language Students in English-Medium Classrooms: A Guide for Teachers in International Schools*, Bristol, UK: Multilingual Matters

Smith, A. and Call, N. (2001) *The Alps Approach Resource Book*, Stafford, UK: Network Educational Press

Smith, A., Lovatt, M. and Wise, D. (2003) *Accelerated Learning: A User's Guide*. Network Educational Press Ltd. https://www.bloomsbury.com/uk/accelerated-learning-a-users-guide-9781855391505/

Swan, M. (1995) *Practical English Usage*, Oxford, UK: Oxford University Press

Swan, M. and Walter, C. (1997) *How English Works: A Grammar Practice Book*, Oxford, UK: Oxford University Press

William, D. (2018) *Embedded Formative Assessment*. Bloomington, IN: Solution Tree

Wilson, J. and Carmel Education Trust. (2014) *Closing the Gap with the New Primary National Curriculum*, Nottingham, UK: National College for Teaching & Leadership

Zadina, J. N. (2014) *Multiple Pathways to the Student Brain*. San Francisco, CA: Jossey-Bass

Vocabulary and grammar list

Vocabulary

add, subtract, times, divide	lesson 7b, 50
animals	lesson 10a, 55
calculations	lesson 7b, 50
clarifying things	pre–induction session A, 19, 22
classroom instructions	pre–induction session F, 19, 29–30
classroom instructions	lesson 4c, 41, 44
colours	lesson 3a, 19, 37
counting 1–10	lesson 2a, 35
counting 1–20	lesson 2b, 19, 35–36
counting 20-39	lesson 7a, 50
counting 20-50	lesson 7a, 7b, 50
descriptions	lesson 15a, 32, 70
directions	lesson 30a, 30b, 21, 118–120
family, extended	lesson 14a, 14b, 20, 67–69
family, immediate	lesson 13a, 13b, 20, 62–66
feelings	pre–induction session B, lesson 28a, 19, 112–114
food	lesson 20b, 84
his, hers, yours, my	lesson 6a, 47–49
hobbies	lesson 19a, 82–83
home	lesson 23b, 95, 100
levels of like	lesson 8a, 51
numbers	lesson 2a, 2b, 7a, 7b, 18a, 19, 35–36, 50, 81
numbers 1–20	lesson 2a, 2b, 19, 35–36
numbers 20-50	lesson 7a, 7b, 50
ordinal numbers	lesson 18a, 81
places	lesson 29a, 115
possessive adjectives: his, hers, yours, my	lesson 6a, 47–49
rooms in the school	pre–induction session D, 26
rooms of the house	lesson 23a, 95
shops	lesson 29a, 115
some	lesson 20a, 84
sports	lesson 16a, 74
subjects, school	pre–induction session C, lesson 8b, 24–25, 51
verbs	lesson 9a, 53
vowels	lesson 4a, 41
wants	lesson 28b, 112

174

Grammar

a/an	lesson 4b, 41
can/can't for ability	lesson 17a, 79–80
can/can't for permission	lesson 25a, 25b, 104–106
can I . . .? yes, you can/ no, you can't.	pre–induction session E, lesson 25a, 26, 104–106
classifiers	lesson 21a, 88–90
do you/does he. . .?	lesson 16b, 26a, 74, 107–108
do you have . . .? yes, I have got . . .	lesson 15b, 15c, 70, 72–73
do you like . . .? yes, I do/no, I don't.	lesson, 8a, 8b, 16b, 51–52, 75, 77
feelings	lesson 28a, 28b, 112–114
greetings	lesson 1a, 32
had got/have got, have not (got)/haven't (got)	lesson 13c, 15b, 15c, 62, 66, 70, 72, 73
have you got. . .?	lesson 20b, 84–87
his, hers, yours, my	lesson 6a, 47–49
how are you? she is. . .	lesson 1b, 32, 34
how many brothers and sisters has he/she got?	lesson 13c, 62, 66
how much/how many . . .	lesson 22a, 92–94
how old are you? I am . . . years old.	lesson 2c, 35–36
I have/haven't got a/an/ some	lesson 21b, 88, 91
I like . . . I don't like . . .	lesson 8a, 51–52
imperatives,	lesson 12a, 60–61
irregular plurals,	lesson 10b, 55, 57
is/are there . . .? there are/aren't/is/isn't,	lesson 23d, 95, 100
is it . . .? yes, it is/no, it isn't.	lesson 3c, 37, 40
likes and dislikes	lesson 8a, 51–52
making friends	lesson 1a, 1b, 32–34
plurals (irregulars)	lesson 10b, 55, 57
possessive adjectives	lesson 6a, 47–48
prepositions	lesson 24a, 101–103
prepositions of place	lesson 29a, 115–117
pronoun plus verb	lesson 9a, 53
she/he can. . .	lesson 17a, 79
she/he has got. . .	lesson 13c, 15b, 15c, 62, 66, 70, 72–73
she/he wants	lesson 28b, 112–114
she/he wants to. . .	lesson 28b, 112–114
subject + verb + object	lesson 9a, 9b, 53–54
there are/aren't/is/isn't	lesson 23c, 23d, 24b, 95–96, 99, 103
this, that, those, these	lesson 5a, 11a, 45–46, 58–59
this is a/an. . .	lesson 10a, 55
verbs	lesson, 9a, 9b, 26a, 16b, 53–54, 74, 77, 107–108
wants	lesson 28b, 112–114
what are these? these are . . .	lesson 11a, 58
what's that in English?	lesson 5a, 45–46
what's this/that? it's a/an. . .	lesson 5a, 45–46
what's your name? my name is. . .	lesson 1a, 33
what would you like? I would like. . .	lesson 27a, 27b, 109–111
where is/are . . .?	lesson 29a, 30b, 115–117, 118–120
who is this? this is. . .	lesson 14a, 14b, 67–69
whose is this/that? this is my/her/his	lesson 6a, 14a, 47, 49, 67–68
would you like . . .? yes, I would/no, I wouldn't	lesson 27a, 27b, 109–111

175

Language structure and vocabulary index

a/an 19, 41–42, 84, 85

auxiliary verbs 37, 51

Adams, Helen 137–138

admission procedures, enhanced 128

adverbs 125

adverbs of frequency 122

animals 20, 55–56

assessment 7–9; baseline 145–157; baseline assessment 7–8; code description 9; in consolidation 6; EAL learners actively involved in 127; evidence used in consolidation 128; learner self-assessment 8; for learning 8; for learning forms 159–162; NASSEA EAL, overview of 163–166; of new-to-English learners 128; of prior knowledge 129; strands and self-assessment questions 128–130; using EAL assessment continuum 8–9

attributes 20

baseline assessment 145–158; answers 157–158; questions 145–156

Basic Interpersonal Communication Skills (BICS) 2

be 37

because, so 125

Bell Foundation 163–166

body 122

buddies 6, 22, 29, 128

building the field, in scaffolding 133

calculations 50

can/can't for ability 79–80

can/can't for permission 21, 104–106

can I . . .? yes, you can/ no, you can't. 19, 21, 28, 104–106

clarifying things 19, 22

Clarke, Joanna 138

classifiers 21, 88–91

classroom 19, 37, 38

classroom instructions 19, 29–30, 41, 44

clothes 121

code description 9; B – early acquisition 9; C – developing competence 9; D – competent 9; E – fluent 9; A – new to English 9

Cognitive Academic Language Proficiency (CALP) 2

collaboration, modes of 133–136

collaborative games for the demonstration phase 15–16

colours 19, 37

Community-Based English Language intervention 138

comparatives 126

consolidation 5–6; assessment 6; cross-curricular links 5–6; reviewing learning 5

countable/uncountable nouns 84, 88

counting 1–10 35

counting 1–20 19, 35–36

counting 20–39 50

counting 20–50 50

cross-curricular links, in consolidation 5–6

cures 123

cycle of learning 4, 9–16; collaborative games for the demonstration phase 15–16; cycle of independent and teacher-supported small-group learning sessions 10; cycle of independent learning sessions 11; cycle of learner-directed learning – further detail 11; cycle of supported learning sessions 10, 11; cycle of teacher-supported small-group learning sessions 15; 4 Stage Accelerated Learning Cycle 4; language structure lesson 14–15; to scaffold writing 133; using lesson flashcard resources with 9; vocabulary lesson 12–13

daily routine 121–122

days of the week 122

descriptions 32, 70

did/didn't 124

differentiation for EAL learners in class 128–129, 131–132

directions 21, 118–120

do you/does he. . .? 21, 74, 77, 107–108

do you have . . .? yes, I have got . . . 21, 70, 72

do you like . . .? yes, I do/no, I don't. 20, 51–52, 74–78

drinks 21

English as an additional language (EAL): introduction to teaching to 7–14-year-olds 1–2; national expectations for EAL learners 2

English as an additional language (EAL) framework 127–136; assessing prior knowledge 129; conclusion 136; guidance on differentiation for EAL learners in class 128–129, 131–132; modes of collaboration 133–136; pre-teaching 132; scaffolding 129, 133; share the rationale 132; strands and self-assessment questions 128–130; use of mother tongue 132; use of substitution tables 132–133; for whole school development 127, 130

English for parents in schools 139–144

English to Speaking of Other Languages (ESOL) 138

families, including 137–144

family, extended 20, 67–69

family, immediate 20, 62–66

family learning 137–138

family learning framework 138, 139–144

feelings 19, 112–114

food 21, 84–85, 88, 92

friends, making 19, 32–34

front-loading 132

greetings 32

had 125

had got/have got, have not (got)/haven't (got) 62, 66, 70, 72

have to/don't have to 125

have you got. . .? 84–87

his, hers, yours, my 20, 47–49

hobbies 21, 82–83

home 21, 95–100

how are you? she is . . . 19, 32, 34

how do you get to 123

how many brothers and sisters has he/she got? he/she has got . . . 20, 62, 66

how much/how many . . . 21, 92–94

how often do you. . .? 122

how old are you? I am . . . years old. 19, 35–36

I have/haven't got a/an/ some 21, 88, 91

illness 123

I like . . . I don't like . . . 20, 51

imperatives 20, 60

independent writing, in scaffolding 133

induction programme 19–126; *see also* pre-induction sessions; animals and plurals 55–57; can/can't for ability 79–80; can/can't for permission 104–106; classifiers 88–91; classroom vocabulary and a/an 41–44; colours and the classroom 37–40; counting 1–20 35–36; description and had got/have got 70–73; details and resources 30; directions 118–126; do you/does he . . .? 107–108; extended family and possessives 67–69; feelings 112–114; have you got . . .? 84–87; his, hers, yours, my 47–49; hobbies 82–83; home and there is/are . . . 95–100; how much/how many . . . 92–94; immediate family and have got/has got 62–66; imperatives 60; induction pathway 31; likes and dislikes 51–52; making friends 19, 32–34; numbers 20–50 50; ordinal numbers 81; overview of 19–21; prepositions 101–103; shops and places 115–117; sports and do you like . . . yes, I do/no, I don't 74–78; subject + verb + object 53–54; this, that, these, those 58–59; vocabulary in English 45–46; would you like . . .? 109–111

induction programme, introduction to 3–18; assessment 7–9; code description 9; guidance on planning and teaching the programme 9–16 (*see also* cycle of learning); how it works – in practice (including assessment) 6–9; how it works – in theory 3–6; activation 5; connection 4–5; consolidation 5–6; cycle of learning 4, 9–16; demonstration 5; strategic, self-regulated language learning 4; non-literate learners 18; Remember Book 6–7; successful lesson, creating 16–18

introductory 19

irregular plurals 55, 57

irregular verbs 124

is/am/are (the verb 'to be') 32, 35

is/are there . . .? there are/aren't/is/isn't 95–96, 99

is it . . .? yes, it is/no, it isn't. 19, 37, 40

jobs 123

joint construction, in scaffolding 129

learning forms, assessment for 159–162

levels of like 20, 51–52

likes and dislikes 20, 51–52

Limited English proficient/English Language Learners (LEP/ELL) 127

making friends 32–34

modal verbs 37, 51

modeling genre, in scaffolding 129

money 121

months 124

mother tongue: in EAL framework 127–130, 132; including families 137, 144; language flashcards and 6; suggestions for making connections with 16–17; to support conceptual learning, importance of 1, 2

must/must not 125

NASSEA EAL assessment overview 163–166

National Curriculum for England 2

national expectations for EAL learners 2
National Learning and Work Institute 138
new-to-English learners 1, 128
non-literate learners 18; reading 18
numbers 19, 20, 35–36, 50
numbers 1–20 19, 35–36
numbers 20–50 50

ordinal numbers 21, 81

parents in schools, English for 139–144
past tense 125
past tense verbs 125
perhaps 126
places 21, 115–117
plurals 55, 57
possessive adjectives: his, hers, yours, my 47
possessive s ('s) 67
pre-induction sessions: can I. . .? 19, 28; clarifying
   things 19, 22; classroom instructions 19, 29;
   feelings 19, 23; overview 19, 22; pre-induction
   language flashcards 22; rooms in the school 19, 26;
   school subjects 19, 24
prepositions 21, 101–103
prepositions of place 115–117
present simple 53
pre-teaching 132
pronoun plus verb 20, 53

Queen Katherine Academy 138
question tags 37, 51

rationale, sharing 132
Remember Book 6–7
reviewing learning, in consolidation 5
Roma families 138
rooms in the school 19, 26
rooms of the house 21, 95–96

scaffolding 4, 129–130, 132–133, 170
s/es/ies/ves 55
session contents: animals and plurals 55–57; can/can't
   for ability 79–80; can/can't for permission 104–106;
   classifiers 88–91; classroom vocabulary and a/an 41–44;
   colours and the classroom 37–40; counting 1–20 35–36;
   description and had got/have got 70–73; details and
   resources 30; directions 118–126; do you/does he
   . . .? 107–108; extended family and possessives 67–69;
   feelings 112–114; have you got . . .? 84–87; his, hers,
   yours, my 47–49; hobbies 82–83; home and there

is/are . . . 95–100; how much/how many . . . 92–94;
   immediate family and have got/has got 62–66;
   imperatives 60; induction pathway 31; likes and dislikes
   51–52; making friends 19, 32–34; numbers 20–50 50;
   ordinal numbers 81; overview of 19–21; prepositions
   101–103; shops and places 115–117; sports and do you
   like . . . yes, I do/no, I don't 74–78; subject + verb +
   object 53–54; this, that, these, those 58–59; vocabulary
   in English 45–46; would you like . . .? 109–111
shape 123
she/he can . . . 20, 79
she/he has got . . . 20, 62, 66, 70–73
she/he is . . . 21
she/he wants . . . 21, 112–114
shops 21, 115–117
small-group support record 168
some 84, 86
sports 20, 74–78
subject + verb + object 20, 53–54
subjects, school 19, 20, 24
substitution tables 129–130, 132–133
successful lesson, creating 16–18; effective planning 17;
   mother tongue 16–17; patience 17; phonics 18; success
   and praise 17; total physical response 18
superlatives 126

there are/aren't/is/isn't 21, 95, 96, 99, 103
there was/were 124
third person 53, 126
this, that, those, these 45–46, 58–59
this is a/an . . . 20, 55
time 121
time indicators 124
time markers 122
time revision 122
to be 37
transport 123

uncountable nouns 92

verbs 20, 37, 51, 53, 74, 77, 107–108, 124
vowels 19, 41

wants 21, 112–114
was/were 124
weather 125
welcome procedure 128
what are these? these are . . . 20, 58
what is he doing? 123
what's going to/will happen? 125–126

what's that in English? 19, 45–46
what's this/that? it's a/an . . . 19, 45–46
what's your name? my name is . . . 19, 33
what would you like? I would like . . . 20, 109–111
where is/are . . .? 21, 115–117, 118–120
who is this? this is . . . 20, 68

whole school EAL development 127, 130
whose is this/that? this is my/her/his 20, 47, 49, 68
why are you going? 123
word order 20, 53
would you like . . .? yes, I would/no, I wouldn't, thank you
    21, 109–111

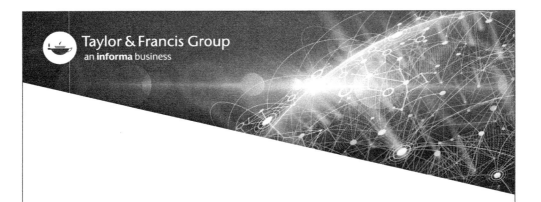